Stuart Robertson's Tips

on

Organic Gardening

~

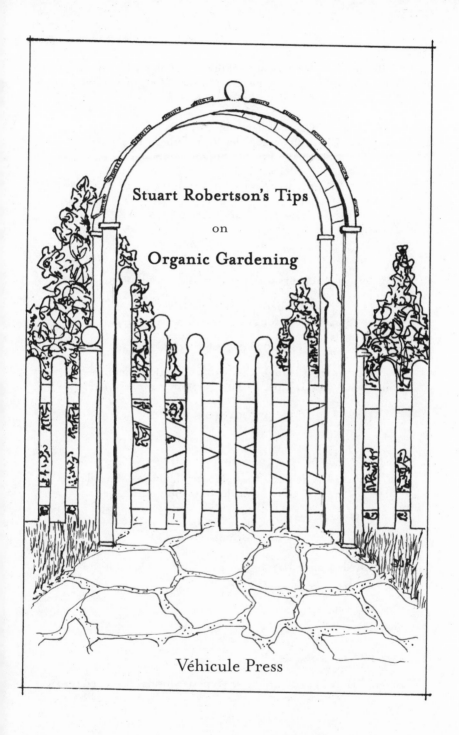

Stuart Robertson's Tips

on

Organic Gardening

Véhicule Press

Published with the assistance of the Book Publishing Industry
Development Program of the Department of Canadian Heritage.

Cover designed by J.W. Stewart
Cover photograph by Stuart Robertston.
Set in Mrs Eaves by Simon Garamond
All drawings by the author
Printed by Marquis Book Printing Inc.

LIBRARY AND ARCHIVES CANADA CATALOGUING IN PUBLICATION

Robertson, Stuart, 1944-
Stuart Robertson's tips on organic gardening.

ISBN 978-1-55065-235-2

1. Organic gardening—Canada. 2. Organic gardening—
Snowbelt States. I. Title. II. Title: Tips on organic gardening.

SB453.5.R63 2007   635'.04840971   C2007-904445-X

Published by Véhicule Press, Montréal, Québec, Canada
www.vehiculepress.com

Distribution in Canada by LitDistCo
orders@litdistco.ca

Distribution in U.S. by Independent Publishers Group
www.ipgbook.com

ContentsPrinted in Canada on 100% post-consumer recycled paper.

I would like to dedicate this book to
William Augustus Robertson, my grandfather, who showed me
what a real gardener can do.

Acknowledgements

Thank you to all the friends and family who over the years have contributed to my love of gardening. And thanks for putting up with my efforts as I learned.

Barry Lazar was the CBC producer who had the courage, first of all to put me on the radio, and then to teach me how it worked. *Gazette* editor Julian Armstrong pushed me to write my first newspaper column, and never stopped encouraging me. Since then, many others have given help and direction as a hobby developed into a career.

Some of the most pleasurable and useful times I have are giving lectures to groups of gardeners, the "talented amateurs" like me who are always willing to try something new and are willing to help others with their successes and failures. I know most of them are better gardeners than I am, but I love it when they pretend otherwise.

My wife Donna deserves a lot of praise for putting up with my aching muscles, buying me all the tools I crave and making me feel as if I know what I'm doing. Her exquisite taste is gradually rubbing off on me. And my son Jeremy was the one who actually pushed me into starting this book, and who let me take the time to do it.

Thank you most of all to the team who took the real risk by agreeing to publish this book. Simon Dardick and Nancy Marrelli at Véhicule Press have supported so many writers over the years, and have stayed cheerfully optimistic throughout the experience. I'm honoured to be one of their latest.

Contents

Introduction

Over the past twenty-six years of writing a gardening column for the *Montreal Gazette*, doing gardening phone-in shows on CBC Radio and giving lectures to all sorts of groups, I've heard a lot of questions.

These questions have always been the basis for the gardening information I try to pass along to people. And it's something that I have a lot of fun doing.

There's no such thing as a "silly question" when it comes to gardening. If you want to ask, it's obviously important to you to get the answer. I still have lots of questions of my own, and the best way to learn the answers is to ask someone about them, or look them up in a book.

Sometimes a question is just a way for two gardeners to get into a discussion about gardening. Perhaps we already have a good answer to our own question, but we might find out something new by asking it anyway. Asking questions seems to be the hallmark of being a gardener.

This book is tailored for the average contemporary gardener, like me, who doesn't want to spend hours slaving away in the garden. We want to get the job done as easily as possible, but of course we also want the best results possible. I didn't set out to write the definitive book on gardening, because I'm sure that's already been done.

This is just a collection of answers to questions. They're ideas for ways of doing things that I've found to work, to be fairly easy to manage and that involve as little work as possible. Since I've always tried to minimize the work-to-pleasure ratio in my gardening efforts, I hope they'll help you get more fun out of gardening. Lots of the ideas in this book came from you over the years anyway, and you may recognize them as the way you do things already. There are always other ways to do things, perhaps better ways than I've described. If they work for you, let me know about them. I'm just trying to help people muddle through the gardening year, equipped with a certain amount of gardening skills, and hoping for great results.

One of the best ways to get good long-term gardening results is to be as organic in your approach as possible. "Going Organic" is more a matter of "thinking organic" than sticking to a hard set of rules. When you have a choice of ways to do something, chose the most natural one, the one with the least negative impact on the environment. You'll find that by minimizing your reliance on products that cost the environment and using organic techniques in stead, you'll actually be maximizing the chances of long-lasting health for your garden.

Today's version of being organic uses many of the oldest gardening techniques around, but it embraces many of the latest products as well. It's heartening to see that so much horticultural and agricultural research is devoted to products and practices that work with the environment rather than against it. Part of this effort is driven because it makes good economic sense, but part of it came about because of the demand from gardeners and consumers to look for alternatives.

It's up to all gardeners to keep asking for these alternatives when shopping for products, and supporting suppliers and retailers who provide them. Non-organic fertilizers and pesticides still account for the lion's share of the market, but that's gradually changing thanks to your pressure. As seen in a province like Quebec, laws governing pesticide use can change. And the industry can change along with it.

So I hope you have fun reading this book, and have fun gardening into the future. It's still perhaps the most popular hobby in North America (next to complaining about the weather) in spite of its minor frustrations. That's because it's also one of the most satisfying.

ONE

Soil

What makes a good soil?

The difference between a good garden and a great garden is in the soil.

Really spectacular results from your plants can only be kept up year after year if they're growing in a healthy environment, and not just because you're feeding them all sorts of fertilizers. Plants are quick to respond to both good and bad growing situations, so it's our job to make sure they always have the best.

Building a good soil is something that you should start working on the minute you take control of your garden. It also has to become part of your regular gardening routine every season. It's not particularly hard work, but it does mean you should understand what's in a good soil and how you can build and maintain it.

What's in a good garden soil?

Good garden soil is made up of just the right combination of the following things:

> *Minerals* (clay, silt and sand) provide inorganic
> nutrients.
> *Organic matter* (decaying animal and vegetable
> matter) provides organic nutrients & humus.
> *Water* supplies hydrogen & liquids for plant
> circulation.
> *Air* once it enters the soil provides oxygen, carbon &
> ammonia.
> *Living organisms.*

We'll deal with how to supply this combination shortly, but first I'd like to underline the importance of those living organisms, the actual life in your soil.

By "life" I mean all the insects, fungi and micro-organisms that live and work in a healthy soil. While they consume, excrete and die they help to break down the mineral and organic matter into a soup that's referred to as "the soil solution." It's this solution of matter and water and air that provides nutrients and fluids to the roots of the plants.

A good soil full of organic matter spawns and encourages this life, and therefore the fertility that comes with it. Conversely, a soil fed with fertilizers made from mineral salts will discourage this life, and over time the vigour and the health of the plants will suffer. It's the difference between an ordinary garden and a great garden.

Why do I have to keep adding organic matter?
The minerals in soil come in the form of sand, silt and clay. They're just different-sized particles of the same basic mix of geological minerals such as quartz and limestone. And because they're minerals, they last a long time.

However, the organic matter in soil is far more volatile. It gets broken down into humus and is consumed very quickly each growing season, and even large amounts of organic matter will disappear into the soil solution between the spring and the fall of each year.

So every year, the soil needs to have its organic matter replenished if you want to maintain the correct balance over the whole season. Spring is the best time of year to add it to the soil of your flower garden, but the heavy feeders in the vegetable garden could do with an application both in the spring and mid summer.

What can I use as organic matter?
The very best source of organic matter is home-made compost. It's usually made from a mixture of fresh kitchen and garden

waste, old leaves, woody stems from plants, animal manures, wood ash and leftover soil from last season's containers. As these things break down during decomposition they release their locked-in nutrients for re-use, so compost becomes a form of fertilizer. By the end of the composting process these ingredients have become a sweet-smelling soil-like material that's full of organic and mineral nutrients, as well as fibres. This mixture helps to improve both the structure and fertility of your soil.

If you don't have your own compost pile, you can buy packages of commercially-made compost. These are made in a similar way, on a much larger scale, using things like waste vegetable matter from municipalities, animal manures and the waste from agricultural and marine food processing.

As well as compost, there are other sources of easy-to-decompose organic matter available that you can add to your soil. For example, shredded leaves, chopped up straw, finely shredded bark, and even shredded coconut husks (coir). These materials can be added directly to the garden soil and blended in. But a much better way to get them into your soil is to include them as part of your compost pile each year. That way they get decomposed quickly and blended in with all the other ingredients.

How can I tell if my soil structure needs improving?

As mentioned, a good gardening soil has to have the right balance of minerals, water and air to go along with the organic matter.

The minerals are a long-term source of nutrients and they also provide a structure for the roots to support the rest of the plant. Water, as well as providing hydrogen, is essential for the dilution of the nutrients in the soil solution and provides the liquid for circulation within the plant. And the air is a critical supplier of elements such as carbon, oxygen and nitrogen from ammonia.

As mentioned before, the minerals are composed of different-sized particles we refer to as sand, silt and clay.[fig. 1] They clump together to form aggregates in the soil, and this construction is very important. A soil composed of only sand allows such fast drainage that plants soon lack water. Soils of pure clay are just the opposite, and hold far too much water for long periods so that plants can drown.

[FIG. 1] THREE PARTICLE SIZES

So as mixtures of sand, silt and clay are stuck together with humus to form aggregates, these clumps are critical to the way the soil performs. They trap the right amount of moisture on their uneven surfaces, and because they're lumpy and leave gaps between them they make up a structure in the soil that allows good drainage and the essential passage of air around the roots.

To quickly find out what the structure of your soil is, you can do one simple test. I call it the Squeeze Test, and it shows which of the three main mineral categories is dominant in your soil.

∼ THE SQUEEZE TEST ∼

You can quickly tell the structure of a damp soil by taking a handful of it and squeezing it into a roll in one hand. When you open your hand, if the soil falls apart all by itself, it's very sandy. If it forms into a heavy wet tube that sticks together, it's heavy clay. If it holds its shape in a roll until you touch it with a finger, and then it breaks apart easily, you've got soil with a well-balanced loamy texture.

To get a much better idea of the actual composition of your garden soil you can try another quick test. It's an unsophisticated home-made analysis that I call the Jar Test, and it shows quite clearly the actual texture of your soil.

∼ THE JAR TEST ∼

You'll need a glass jar that holds a couple of litres, like a big pickle jar. Take a sample of your garden soil and dump it into the jar until it's about one-third full. Then fill up the jar with tap water. Put the lid on the jar, and shake the whole thing until the soil and water mix completely.

Now comes the analysis part. As soon as you stop shaking the jar, put it down and watch what happens. All the components of the soil have been broken up, and are spinning around. As the spinning slows, the components will settle, starting with the heaviest and finishing with the lightest. [fig. 2]

Right away you'll see the heavy sand particles settle to the bottom. After five or ten minutes you'll see the slightly lighter silt particles have formed a layer on top of the sand. The water will still be all muddy looking, so leave the jar overnight.

In the morning you'll see that a third layer of very lightweight clay particles has settled out of the water on top of the silt. The water will be much clearer, and you'll notice a bunch of loose stuff floating on the top of the water. This is organic matter, like fibre and bits of plant material.

Now you've got a visual representation of your soil's structure in the jar, and you can actually measure it. The sand is at the bottom, then the silt, with the clay on top. What are your proportions of sand to silt to clay? They should be about equal amounts, about 30% of each. A good soil should also have a layer of organic matter floating on the top that's about 10% of the total.

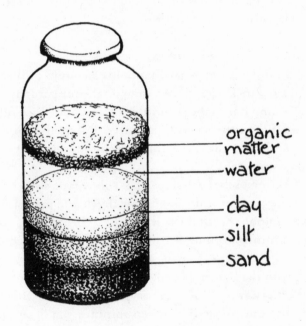

organic matter
water
clay
silt
sand

[FIG. 2] THE BOTTLE TEST

How can I improve the structure of my soil?

Once you've done a test, you'll have a good idea of what to add to your soil to get the right balance of ingredients, and to have the structure that you want.

The two extreme conditions of imbalance in a soil are too much fine clay or too much loose sand. You can tell a lot about the structure and composition of your garden's soil by just observing the way water behaves on it. After a heavy rain, if you see water staying on the surface for a long time then you know it's got a lot of clay in it. If it drains quickly and is always dry and in need of water, then there's probably too much sand.

Improving either a heavy clay soil or a sandy soil has one thing in common. Both conditions are improved with the addition of humus, or decomposed organic matter. You can add almost any type of organic matter to help this situation but the best source is from compost, either purchased in a bag, or from your own pile.

For a sandy soil, the minerals and organic matter in the compost hold the water better and help to make a good moist home for roots. For an extremely sandy soil you should add a plentiful annual application of compost, shredded leaves and any other organic matter you can lay your hands on.

For heavy clay soils, the compost works in the opposite way to achieve the same end. The minerals and organic matter from the compost break up the tiny tightly-packed clay particles into larger lumps. This makes a soil that drains better, allows air to circulate and lets the roots grow more easily. Clay soils are also improved by adding materials such as shredded dried leaves, very finely shredded wood or equal amounts of compost and peat. Adding copious amounts of sand or perlite also helps. Two other items to add to a clay soil are calcium and gypsum, as they chemically assist the "lumping" process along. You can buy bags of a special soil improvement product such as "Clay-Breaker," which is usually composed of peat and wood fibres, along with some gypsum.

You can buy bags of sand and you can buy bags of heavy clay soil, but where do you get silt? The best way to increase the silt content of your soil is to add gravel dust or grit, which is usually available from building-supply companies.

Do different plants need different types of soils?

The ideal structure and texture for a garden soil depends a bit on what you're growing in it. For the sake of description, soils are classified with names that relate to their texture, based on their different mixtures of the three mineral sizes (clay, silt and sand).

Annual and perennial flowers do best in a soil described as "loam," which has 20% clay, 40% silt and 40% sand. It's quite light in weight and easy to work.

Most large vegetables are heavy feeders, and they need more available minerals from a soil that's referred to as "silty clay loam." It has 30% clay, 60% silt and 10% sand.

Smaller leafy vegetables prefer a well-drained "silty loam", which is composed of 20% clay, 60% silt and 40% sand.

In all of these classes of soil, the other essential ingredient is always organic matter. As mentioned in the "Jar Test," it should be about 10% of the total mineral content.

There are some plants that have very distinct preferences in soil type, and of course they'll do better if you provide it for them.

∾ PLANT SOIL PREFERENCES ∾

Plants preferring the moistness of a "clay loam"
(40% clay, 50% silt, 10% sand)

Anemone japonica, asclepias, caltha, chrysanthemum, cimicifuga, helenium, hemerocallis, hibiscus, iris versicolor, lobelia, lysimachia, lythrum, monarda, myosotis, trollius, ferns, ornamental grasses, the large vine crops (squash, melon, cucumber, pumpkin) and cole crops (cabbage, cauliflower, broccoli).

Plants preferring a well-draining "silty loam"
(20% clay, 60% silt, 40% sand)
Alpines and perennial herbs.

Plants preferring a drier "sandy loam"
(10% clay, 40% silt, 50% sand)
Achillea, ajuga, anthemis, arabis, aster, aubretia, centurea, coreopsis, delphinium, dianthus, digitalis, dimorphotheca, echinops, gallardia, helianthus, ipomea, bearded iris, kochia, liatris, mesembryanthemum, mirabilis, papaver, phlox, portulaca, rudbeckia, salvia, sanvitalia and zinnia, bulb plants, annual herbs, perennial vegetables such as asparagus and rhubarb, and the root vegetables.

How important is the pH of my soil?

Once you've got a good soil structure, it's important that all the nutrients in it are available to the plants.

The pH level refers to how acid or alkaline your soil is, and the pH level can have a bearing on whether nutrients will be chemically available to your plants or not.

The pH scale runs from 0.0 to 14.0, with 7.0 considered as neutral. Below 7.0 is acid, and above is alkaline. Very small changes in pH represent large differences. A change of one number, for instance from 6.0 to 5.0, means the pH is 10 times as acid. [fig. 3]

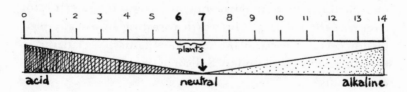

[fig. 3] pH TEST

A pH in the neutral area will ensure that the mineral nutrients in the soil are soluble, and that the organisms are active in the soil, releasing the organic nutrients. However, if the pH is too acid or too alkaline many of the nutrients will be locked up and unavailable to the plant, even if you've added lots of fertilizer.

Most of the decorative and vegetable plants that we grow are happiest when the pH is in the range from 6.0 to 7.0, or nearly neutral. And fortunately for us gardeners, a soil with a good organic and mineral ratio usually falls within this range.

It's rare that the pH of a garden soil gets more acid or alkaline than this, unless some outside influences have affected it. For instance, the soil around a home that's just had some construction done might have traces of acid or alkaline products that have been used in the building process, so it's worth testing certain sections. Homes located close to heavy industry may also suffer from precipitation which is not neutral, and tests of your surface soil are a good idea.

How can I test my soil's pH?
There are pH tests you can do at home, and they're fairly accurate. But there are usually two levels of test kits sold in stores or through catalogues, and it's only the more expensive ones using laboratory-grade chemicals that are worth buying. They measure the colour of liquid run-off from your small soil sample against a colour-coded chart.

If plants are mysteriously dying in one area of your garden, or something in your environment has given you cause for concern, then it might be worth investing in a really professional lab analysis of the soil. Companies specializing in this are usually listed under "Soil analysis" or "Environmental consultants".

What pH level do plants prefer?
As mentioned before, most garden plants prefer a neutral or slightly alkaline soil pH between 6.0 and 7.0. There are a few

plants that prefer to grow in a "slightly" acid soil, and I emphasise *slightly*. It should have a pH of between 5.5 and 6.5.

Some of the more popular acid-loving plants are ornamentals such as aconitum (monkshood), azalea, baptisa, cimicifuga, convallaria (lily-of-the-valley), coreopsis, dicentra, liatris, gentian, phlox, ranunculus (buttercup), rhododendron and viburnum.

To increase the acidity of a soil you can add products such as sulphur, ferrous sulphate or aluminium sulphate. It takes about two pounds per 100 square feet to lower the pH by one. You can also mix large quantities of peat or shredded oak leaves into the soil to increase its acidity.

If a soil tends to become too acid, horticultural lime can be added to make it more alkaline and bring it back to neutral. Most vegetables prefer a pH between 6.5 and 7.0, so lime should be added to the soil if it's below that.

There are very few plants that are comfortable growing in an alkaline soil with a pH above 7.3, and fortunately not many garden soils get this way.

How can I tell the fertility of my soil?

Knowing the composition and pH of your soil still doesn't tell you if it's as full of nutrients as you'd like. Your soil's fertility depends on how well the minerals and organic matter are breaking down in the soil solution and are available to the plant's roots.

You can get a fertility test done by a laboratory, but testing is expensive for the home gardener and not of much use when the analysis tells you how many tons per acre of certain nutrients to add!

There are soil fertility test kits sold in stores, but in my experience they are horribly inaccurate, with a margin of error that's greater than the adjustments you might need to make.

Going by experience, I've found that the average home

garden can be relied upon to be quite fertile, without any testing, as long as certain procedures are followed. For the observant gardener, your plants will actually be one of the first things to tell you if your soil is not fertile.

If it's just low in fertility you'll notice that growth is slow, the size and quantity of leaves will be poor, and you won't have as many flowers as you'd expect. If there's a serious nutrient deficiency you'll see some signs. Look for tips or edges of leaves burning, leaves becoming pale with darker veins and leaves that turn an unnaturally dark colour.

How can I improve the fertility of my soil?

As long as you've made sure that the ratio of minerals and organic matter in your soil is balanced to what your plants need, and as long as you've been adding organic matter on a regular basis, then your soil is very likely to be quite fertile.

On top of this, you can always add fertilizers to specific areas or plants to ensure that their special needs are taken care of throughout the growing season. I'd highly recommend that you use fertilizers from organic sources for this purpose, as I'll explain in Chapter 3.

What about adding manure to my soil to make it better?

As will be mentioned in Chapter 2 on composting, animal manures are a very useful source of organic matter and nutrients for the garden. But they must be handled with respect.

Manures have been used in horticulture and agriculture from almost the first moment humans started to grow things deliberately, and they are finding increasing popularity again in modern agriculture.

Fresh farm manures from cattle, horses, sheep or poultry usually have a high urine content. This is good, because urine contains large amounts of very soluble nutrients. But it can leach out unless it's mixed with plenty of wood shavings or straw bedding, which soaks up the liquid.

This blend of fresh manure and urine is quite a potent mixture, with a high moisture content. If it's added directly onto the soil of the garden, the nitrogen in the fresh manure being very soluble will leach out quite quickly, and may raise nitrate levels to almost toxic amounts. The highly soluble ammonia in the urine will also flow downwards into the root area, and in such high quantities it's quite likely to burn the plants' roots. This is particularly true of poultry manure, which is the "hottest" or richest in nutrients, and should never be used directly on the garden around plants.

So the best advice about using fresh manure is to cycle it through your compost pile first, and not to use it directly on the soil. That way you get the benefits of what's in the manure, without any of the risks.

Sometimes you can obtain older manure, which has sat in a pile for a year or more. This is much less risky to use on the garden, as it has already lost some of its chemical strength. But just in case, it's still best to take advantage of it as the activator layer in your compost pile.

When should I add things to improve the structure or fertility of my soil?

Soil improvement is an on-going operation, and it can be done any time it's needed. But traditionally a lot of things like compost, fertilizer and soil improvement products such as sand or clay-breaker are added in the very early spring so that the garden benefits from them during its peak growing time.

A word of warning. You have to take care when working on a garden in the early spring, as the ground is still in the process of warming up and drying out from the winter freeze. The top few inches of the soil may have thawed, but below that may be still quite hard. This slows the drainage of any water from snow or rain, and makes the ground mushy.

It's a very bad idea to walk on soil when it's in this condition, as you're bound to compact it when it's wet. The loose soil structure you've worked so hard to achieve can be lost by careless trampling on soggy soil. So try to stay to the sides, or lay a wide board on the lawn and soil to spread your weight. Better still, wait until you see that the soil has thawed and drained to a depth of several inches before you start working on it. See how far you can push a metal rod into the soil, and that will tell you how well the ground is thawing.

Spread all the items you want to add to your soil first, *then* incorporate them into the soil all at once. For an empty vegetable or flower bed, you can use a garden fork to loosen the soil and let everything mix together. However, in an area around existing perennials or shrubs you can't dig deeply for fear of disturbing their roots. So I'd advise using a garden rake, a cultivator or just the tips of a fork to loosen the top couple of inches of soil and let the added ingredients trickle down into the upper level of the soil. Over time, the soil organisms and rainwater will do the job of mixing them up.

You can also spread soil improvement materials in the fall, when you put the garden to bed. By then you'll have seen the garden's performance, and have a good idea of which areas need improving.

As you do this "improvement" procedure each season, your garden soil will gradually improve to deeper depths, and your plants will respond with improved growth.

What is mulching, and why should I do it?
Mulch is just a top dressing that covers the exposed surface of the soil.

It can be made of something that will add nutrients to the soil, such as compost. But it can also be made of a material that is inert, such as plastic. The ancient Chinese used to place flat stones around plants as a decorative mulch.

Mulching is perhaps the single most labour-saving technique that a gardener can practice.

First of all, covering any exposed soil around plants with a barrier of mulch traps the moisture that's already in the soil and keeps it there. It protects the soil from the drying effects of the wind and sun, which on a warm day can very quickly suck the moisture out of the top several inches of the soil.

Secondly, it keeps the surface of the soil underneath from forming a hard crust. This crusty layer can prevent water from penetrating into the soil and getting down to the root area, and the subsequent water run-off contributes to serious soil erosion.

Thirdly, and perhaps most importantly to the home gardener, a layer of mulch is a great protection against weeds. The mulch barrier stops any drifting weed seeds from landing in a hospitable environment and taking root, and by cutting off the light to the soil surface it also hinders the germination of weeds seeds that are already in the soil. [fig.4]

A garden with fewer weeds is a much healthier garden, with less competition for the available nutrients and moisture. And a weed-free garden means a lot less work for the gardener throughout the season.

If you use mulch, you'll be cutting down on two of the most repetitive and time-consuming jobs in gardening; watering and weeding. And you'll be protecting all of those improvements that you've made to your soil.

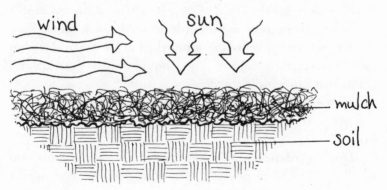

[FIG. 4]MULCH LAYER

What makes a suitable mulch?

Mulch just has to form an effective barrier as described above, so there are many things that can be used.

The most common is a loose layer of organic material that will resist the wind and stay in place. It should allow the downward passage of air and water through it and will gradually decompose to add its goodness to the soil underneath.

Typical organic mulches are straw, chopped leaves, grass clippings, cocoa bean hulls, bark chunks and various organic wastes such as hops from the brewing industry, shredded newspaper, sawdust and small wood chips.

My favourite mulch for the flower garden is shredded cedar bark, which is inexpensive, spreads easily, is a pleasant natural colour and gradually decomposes into the soil.

If you plan to use shredded newspaper, you can use the coloured pages now as well, since newspapers use organic-based inks these days. If you're using sawdust or small wood chips, make sure you spread some nitrogen fertilizer underneath first, as these products will consume nitrogen as they break down. For the same reason, any shredded bark should be cedar or some other softwood because hardwood bark takes up a lot of nitrogen during decomposition.

It's easy to see the effect of pine needles as a natural mulch under evergreen trees, as very little grows through them. They can be gathered and used as a mulch, but be aware that they cause quite an acid soil pH. They should only be used around plants that can handle this.

There are other more solid types of mulch available, some that are completely inorganic rather like the Chinese layer of stones.

Home gardeners and market growers are using more and more sheets of black plastic mulch these days, but because it's not very attractive it's usually relegated to the vegetable garden. The best kind of plastic mulch is dark, to stop weed seeds from germinating in the light, and it should have tiny holes prepunched across it to allow some water and air to penetrate though it.

Make sure to water the soil well first, then spread the sheet tightly over the soil and weigh down the sides with soil or large stones. You can cut slits in the plastic to plant right through it.

Some experimenting has been done with coated reflective film, to raise the early spring air temperature over the mulch for crops such as tomatoes and peppers. In the vegetable garden I've had good results with a red plastic mulch that apparently deters aphids, and also contributes to earlier and more prolific tomato flower production.

Landscape cloth is another man-made fabric that works well as a permanent mulch, and it has the advantage of being slightly porous and lets moisture and air penetrate to the soil underneath. It also needs to be anchored in place over damp soil.

Several sheets of wet newspaper or tar paper make an effective but rather unattractive mulch in the vegetable garden, and I've heard of people using layers of thick cotton fabric as well. Worn-out designer sheets might be just the thing for the garden.

One thing you should never ever use as a mulch is peat moss. I know it's organic and full of fibres, but if you've ever had to deal with peat moss that has completely dried out you've realized that it's almost impossible to re-wet it. The only effective way to dampen dry peat moss is by pouring hot water over it in a container and stirring it up. If you use a layer of peat moss as a mulch on the garden and it dries out, water will run off it like a cement path and never penetrate to the soil underneath.

Very large pieces of bark chunks are used as a decorative type of mulch, but they are best only in certain limited circumstances. Because they are a lot more expensive than most of the other mulches mentioned, the tendency is not to use a very thick layer of them, and this defeats the purpose of having a mulch because they spread apart and let weeds take hold. Bark chunks are most effective if a thin layer of them are laid over a sheet of landscape cloth or plastic to hide it. This is often done around specimen trees or shrubs as a decorative element.

How should mulch be laid?
Mulch should be used to cover all the exposed soil surfaces in your garden., literally anywhere that you want to retain the moisture and avoid weeds. In my experience, that's just about everywhere in the garden!

If you're spreading a loose mulch, there's no point in doing it unless you put down a thick layer. A two inch layer should be the minimum, as it will compact a little with time and the action of the rain on it.

You can even re-spread more mulch later in the season if necessary.

Mulch should be spread to cover the soil right over the root area of plants, but you should leave a couple of inches directly around the base of the plant uncovered. It's best to allow the root crown, where the stems emerge, be exposed to good air circulation, which avoids excessive dampness that might cause damage.

Always water the soil well before you apply any type of mulch, so the moisture is well-established in the soil before it's covered.

It's also a good idea to remove any perennial weeds, roots and all, before you mulch as they will probably push their way up through it anyway. Annual weeds can be knocked down and smothered with the mulch, and they'll just die off.

When is the best time to mulch the garden?
Mulch should be applied as early as possible in the season so that weed seeds are blocked from germinating. However, you must give the soil a chance to warm up in the late winter and very early spring, and a heavy layer of mulch will interfere with warming.

This warming process is very important, as it lets the soil thaw completely and allows any excess moisture to drain away. A dry soil heats up faster than a wet one, so good drainage is essential. The earlier the soil warms, the sooner you'll see perennials responding and the sooner you'll be able to plant in it.

When asked how to tell if the soil is warm, the story goes that a farmer in Norfolk explained his own method of telling when he could plant his seeds.

"Oi takes down me trousers, and zits on the zoil. If I can zit fer foive minuts, it's worm enuf!"

Rather that suggesting you do this in your own garden, I'd recommend using a soil thermometer to show when the soil temperature has reached a suitable level of around 15 C (60F). At that point, you should spread your mulch to conserve moisture and hinder the weeds.

One exception to this rule (there are always exceptions) is when using dark plastic in your vegetable garden. The dark colour of the film actually absorbs the heat of the sun's rays, so the sooner you lay it on the soil surface, the sooner it will heat up. The film also traps the heat in the soil during those cold nights of late winter and very early spring, so you don't lose all the heat gained during the day time.

What is "winter mulching"?
As opposed to spreading mulch in the early part of the season to conserve moisture and reduce weed activity, winter mulching has a very different purpose.

During our winters, there may be times when temperatures rise and we experience periods of alternate freezing and thawing. This cycle causes movement in the soil, and the expanding and contracting can actually cause newly-planted plants to be eased or heaved out of their planting holes.

So if you've disturbed the soil in the fall by planting spring bulbs, perennials or shrubs, the soil over the root areas of these plants should be protected.

31

By spreading a winter mulch you're not trying to keep the soil warm. Quite the opposite. You're trying to keep it frozen hard during those freeze/thaw cycles.

So spread your winter mulch only when the ground has frozen hard. When you can walk on it and it feels like cement, that's the time to spread a couple of inches of a loose organic mulch of the types suggested earlier in this chapter.

What's the best way to make a new planting bed?
Making a new flower or vegetable bed can be a bit of hard work, but it can also be very satisfying because you're able to make a bed entirely to your own specifications.

It's best to do this work in the latter part of the season, because in the spring the soil is wet and very heavy to dig.

My system is a variation of the traditional "double-digging" method, but I've adapted it to the realities of the modern gardener. [fig.5]

First of all, remove any small plants or perennial weeds from the new planting area. If you're making the new bed in what is currently a lawn, leave the grass because it will be useful.

Mark out the area with string on pegs if it's straight-sided, or with a garden hose if it's a free-form shape.

Working across the narrow width, start at one end and dig out a trench with a spade. The trench should be almost as deep as the spade (about 8-10 inches), and a foot wide. Put the removed topsoil from the first trench (including the turf if it's a lawn area) into a barrow and wheel it to the far end of the area for use later.

Use a garden fork to loosen the soil at the bottom of the trench to the full depth of the fork's tines. Then amend the lower soil by throwing in a layer of organic matter. It can be compost, leaf mold, shredded leaves or chopped straw, and you should fill about half the depth of the trench. Add a handful of granular organic fertilizer every foot along the trench.

Then move to the next section, always working by standing

on the old area and not the new bed. Again, dig out a trench from the topsoil, one spade deep and a foot wide. But this time, turn each clod of topsoil (and lawn) upside down and dump it into the first trench.

This way, you've created a new section that has a good deep organic base, with topsoil in the upper section where the plant's roots will be. And if it's lawn that you're digging out, by turning it upside down the grass gets buried and decomposes nicely.

You continue to do this digging/forking/amending operation, trench by trench, until you reach the far end of the new bed where you left your barrow filled with the first trench's removed topsoil. Use that topsoil to fill the upper level of the last trench.

[FIG. 5] DOUBLE DIGGING A NEW BED

You've just built yourself a great new planting bed. You'll notice that the area is probably a few inches higher than before you started, but that's good. A slightly raised bed is preferred, because it will drain and warm up faster in the spring than the surrounding area.

You're now ready to plant in your new bed. You can always add more amendments such as compost as you dig each new planting hole. And you should continue to improve the soil each season as described in this chapter.

TWO

Composting

Compost. Black gold. It's been used by gardeners and farmers to improve their soil from ancient Greek and Roman times, right up until today. With the focus by gardeners on more environmentally sound practices, making and using compost is enjoying a revival in interest.

What is compost?

It's perhaps the oldest type of recycling, where animal and vegetable waste is decomposed to get it back into a form that's usable on the garden, full of nutrients and soil-improving fibres. It's a way of giving back to the soil some of the things that were taken out of it by hungry plants and animals.[fig. 6]

[FIG. 6] GENERIC COMPOST PILE

Why make compost?

Composting is a way of returning to the garden much of the material that came from it in the first place. Think of all the lawn clippings and general waste that you make during the growing season, and all the stuff you cut out of the garden at the end of the season. This is material that otherwise would end up in a landfill site, creating pollution.

Compost also does some wonderful things when it's added to the soil of the garden, by helping to build a good soil structure. As compost breaks down in the soil it provides a sort of glue called humus to help the particles of sand, silt and clay to clump together into those all-important aggregates mentioned in Chapter One. The right soil structure has passages for water and air to flow deeply into the soil, while holding back a suitable amount of moisture for the plants. And this same crumbly structure is ideal for small and large roots to penetrate in search of food and moisture.

Compost also provides nutrients to those roots. The animal, plant and mineral ingredients of the compost have been broken down into a soluble form, which can quickly be broken down even further into the molecules of nutrients needed by plants. The good soil structure also helps to feed the plants, by permitting good aeration to provide oxygen, nitrogen and carbon to the roots.

Compost also provides conditions for an important chemical reaction to take place in your soil. Negatively-charged humus particles attract positively-charged mineral particles, and they bind together. This ability to hold minerals helps to maintain your soil's fertility, even when exposed to the leaching action of water. Soil with lots of organic matter has a scientific basis for being more fertile than soil treated only with artificial fertilizer.

How does a compost pile work?

There are two main types of composting, "hot" and "cold."

The commercial type of large compost pile works because it's a "hot" compost. Chemically active materials such as fresh manure are used in its layered construction, and it gets lots of oxygen during the frequent turning and aeration operations. This makes it heat up and decompose in a matter of days rather than weeks. In fact a "hot" pile will heat up to around 45 to 70 degrees C (115 to 160F), which is enough to kill most weed seeds and pathogens.

The smaller home-style "cold" compost bins don't rely on heat for decomposition. They take a bit longer, but their decomposition relies mainly on microbial and insect activity, and they don't need to be turned as frequently.

How do I set up a compost pile?
First you need something in which to make your compost. For a small property, particularly in a city, there are several varieties of patented composting boxes that are the most sensible to use. They are either round or square, about four feet high and a couple of feet wide with air slots in the sides. They have a top that lifts off to add materials, and a small door near the bottom for access to the finished product. [fig. 7]

The cost of this type of small unit should be under $100, and many municipalities subsidize their purchase to encourage a home-composting program.

There are also cylindrical rotating compost bins which are set up on rollers, and which if used properly can make finished compost in much less time than the static ones. [fig 8.] You jut open a door on the top and drop in the waste as often as you have it.

I've found these rotating systems have a couple of draw-backs. First of all, you have to add an equal amount of dry materials to the container every day, along with the kitchen waste, to keep the whole mixture from getting too soggy. And secondly, it's critical that you do a daily rotation of the composter to tumble the contents and keep them aerated and

[FIG. 7] COMPOST BOXES

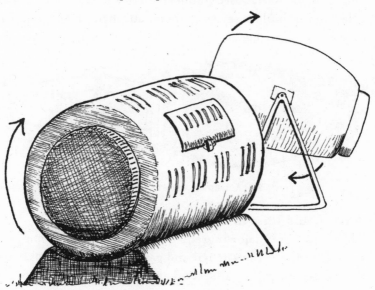

[FIG. 8] ROTATING COMPOSTERS

decomposing properly. If either of these things is not done, the pile becomes anaerobic (lacking air) and starts to smell. This type of composter also has to be emptied completely when you want to get at the finished compost, which can be messy and time-consuming.

For a larger property with larger quantities of waste to dispose of, a larger compost pile will be needed. It can be made as an open pile but it's much more efficient, as well as neater, to set up larger compost enclosures. [fig. 9]

The most common are built with spaced slats of wood to form a structure with plenty of air spaces. You can also use cement construction blocks, and turn them so that the central holes allow the air to pass from the outside into the pile.

The pile should be about four feet square, with a similar height. If you need more volume than one enclosure can provide you can build a series of them, attached or not, and fill each one as it's needed.

[FIG. 9] LARGER COMPOSTING ENCLOSURES

What should I use to make compost?

There are three major ingredient groups for a good compost pile. The first is the kitchen and garden waste that makes up the bulk of the pile. The second are the activators, like soil or manure, that contain masses of the micro-organisms that are going to do all of the work in the pile. The third group are what I call the mineral extras, things like wood ash, lime or granite dust that add nutrients that are not as plentiful in the other ingredients.

The waste provides the raw material, the activators provide the work, and the minerals provide a variety of additional nutrients. The more varied type of ingredients you use in making your compost, the more nutrients will be available to the plants in your garden.

All of the ingredients in your pile will decompose much faster if they are in small sizes. Get into the habit of chopping up things like cantaloupe rinds as you throw them into your under-the-sink compost collector, as this saves time and mess later. You can do the same with garden waste as you collect it. The smaller the pieces of waste, the faster it becomes compost.

It's also a good idea to provide a way of collecting your kitchen and garden wastes that's convenient and secure. In the kitchen you can collect your "compost garbage" in a sturdy plastic bag or lidded container, and empty it often to avoid unpleasant smells. In the garden you can pile assorted plant waste and other things you want to add in bags or containers for use as needed.

Here is a selection of the good and bad ingredients for a typical home compost pile.

~

LIST OF GOOD COMPOST INGREDIENTS

~

Kitchen Waste
Leftover cooked or raw vegetables
Mushrooms
Skins, peelings, cores of vegetables
Breads, pastas, cereal grains, dry or cooked
Undecorated cake, biscuits, crackers
Coffee grains, tea leaves (avoid tea bags and coffee filters)
Animal & human hair

Garden Waste (with no pesticides)
Grass clippings, lawn edgings
Dried shredded leaves
Small twigs and branches, chopped small
Annual weeds, without seeds
Leaves & stems from annuals & perennials
Hedge clippings
Houseplants
Container soil
Loose soil

Other Useful Waste
Seaweed
Hops
Used peat moss
Shredded natural fibres (even clothing)
Shredded newspaper
Small amounts of wood chips & sawdust

LIST OF BAD COMPOST
INGREDIENTS
~

Kitchen waste with creamy sauces
Milk products
Meats, fats, oils, bones
Vinegar, salad dressing
Any garden waste sprayed with pesticide
Weeds with seeds
Roots of perennial weeds
Large diameter woody branches
Large quantities of wood chips & sawdust
Domestic animal waste & litter

How do I build a compost pile?

Whether you're making compost in a box or a larger enclosure system, the pile should be built in the same way, taking advantage of the "layer cake" effect. The bottom of your pile should be sitting on the bare earth, which will allow for good drainage and will gradually attract worms and beneficial organisms into the pile.

A compost pile should be made of thin alternating layers of the three major ingredient groups described before; waste, activators and minerals. This allows the materials to be exposed to each other in small enough quantities to decompose effectively at all levels. [fig. 10]

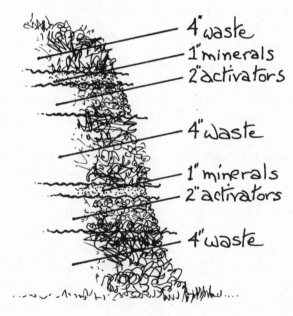

4" waste
1" minerals
2" activators

4" waste

1" minerals
2" activators

4" waste

[FIG. 10] COMPOST LAYER CAKE

Waste

The first layer should be about four inches of your kitchen and garden waste, chopped and shredded into small pieces to decompose better.

Just a quick note about grass clippings. They can be left on the lawn to decompose naturally and benefit the soil right away. However, if you're collecting the clippings for the compost, don't put them all in the composter right away. A thick layer of grass clippings tends to be very wet, and it just makes for a very soggy layer. You can do two things to avoid this. You can leave the clippings on the lawn to dry before you collect them for the compost. Or you can pile them beside your composter and add them a thin layer at a time along with other drier ingredients such as shredded dried leaves. It's a good idea to keep a couple of bags of dried leaves from the autumn near your composter to be used for this purpose. A good balance between wet and dry materials makes for a better pile.

Activators

The second layer in your compost "layer cake" is of activators. This can be any kind of soil, animal manure or even partly decomposed compost from another pile. Spread about an inch or two of activator on top of the waste, so that it's completely covered.

You can throw any kind of uncontaminated soil into your compost. Recycling through the composter is a great way to magically renew poor soil, or to use soils from lawn edgings, old bits of sod or the soil mixes from containers.

Manures really are the key ingredients in making a fast acting and balanced compost. Their high bacterial content is exceptional at increasing the decomposition rate of your pile.

However, getting access to farm manure is not as easy as it was, unless you make frequent visits to farming areas. If you can get hold of cow, horse, sheep or poultry manures and the urine-soaked straw wastes that usually go with it, shovel it onto double plastic bags and store it beside your composter. Fresh manure is not good to use directly on the garden, so it's much better to cycle it through a compost pile first.

If you can't get farm manure, you can always buy bags of

pre-composted manures at garden centres, and these are just as suitable to use in the activator layer of your compost pile.

Minerals

Finally, the third layer of your pile, the sort of icing on the cake, is composed of any minerals that you want to add to the mix to make it better. Most of the ingredients used so far have been very rich in carbon and nitrogen, which are the most important nutrients needed by your plants. But if you're growing a lot of flowers and flowering vegetables then you should also include phosphor and potassium in your compost, along with minor nutrients such as calcium and magnesium.

I would suggest sprinkling a light dusting of horticultural lime powder, just to add some calcium and magnesium. Phosphor can be provided from a handful of rock phosphate or bonemeal. Finally, the potassium needed is available in a handful of granite dust or ground basalt, or about a coffee tin full of wood ash.

Having done your first three layers, you then start with another layer of waste, of activator, of minerals, and keep making these layers until you've used up your supply of waste. You may only make a couple of layers at first, but as the season progresses you'll be adding more waste. And every time you've put about four inches of it on the pile, add the next layers of activators and minerals. Whether you're using a small compost box or several larger enclosures, this layering system is one of the most effective and least time-consuming ways of turning all of your waste into black gold.

So to recap the layer cake system, it's four inches of waste, then two inches of activators followed by a thin layer of minerals.

Building a leaf mold pile.

Leaf mold is a rather special type of compost. You'll find it in nature if you're wandering through a deciduous forest. Dig down under the top leaf layer, and underneath you'll find it turns into a dark crumbly soil, with a wonderful earthy smell. That's leaf mold. Nature makes it all the time. The leaves fall in the forest each year, they rot down into this soil-like consistency, and give back their nutrients to the roots of the tree where they came from. What a nice neat natural cycle.

We can take advantage of this too by making a leaf composter for the fall leaves.[fig. 11] The simplest one of all is to use chicken wire and four wooden or metal stakes to make a cylindrical container. Cut a three–foot wide roll of chicken wire into a length of 12.5 feet. This is enough to make a circular tube four feet across. Use the stakes to hold the wire cylinder in place.

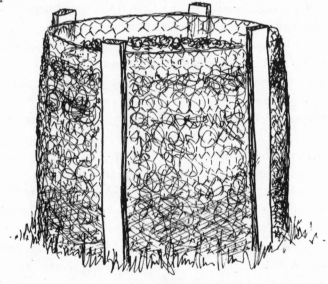

[FIG. 11] LEAF MOLD COMPOSTER

Fill the wire composter with about two feet of dried leaves, then shovel in a couple of inches of soil that will flatten the leaves down. Keep adding two feet of leaves and two inches of soil until the wire composter is just about overflowing. You can set up these inexpensive leaf mold makers all over the place in a forest, or wherever you have room for them.

Leave the pile to work slowly over the next year or two, and you'll gradually see the leaves settle and shrink in volume as they're consumed by the organisms and by decay. Eventually you'll be able to shovel out barrow loads of completed black crumbly leaf mold, which is a very rich source of fibre and nitrogen.

How much work is involved in making compost?

If you've used the triple layer method of building your compost pile, the worms and micro-organisms are going to be doing most of the work for you. They will be most active when the outside temperatures are warm, so it's a good idea to have your pile ready in the late fall or early spring to take advantage of the warmth of the summer.

You can leave the pile alone all summer, just topping it with new layers.

Meanwhile, deep below, the layers you built up are gradually being turned into a black crumbly compost. You can check to see how things are doing towards the late summer. Carefully open the door in the base of the compost box, or remove the front wall of your enclosure. From the very base of the pile you should be able to dig out a shovel full of compost. In fact you may be pleasantly surprised to see just how much of the bottom half of the pile has already turned into something that looks much more like soil than all the junk you threw in there. You'll see that it actually works!

At this point you can remove as much of the finished product as possible, to make way to add more on top. If you keep all the heavy plastic bags that mulch and other garden products come in, you can use them to store your compost as you remove it. As you remove material from the bottom, the pile will finally collapse upon itself, but just leave it for now.

At the end of the summer or in the early fall, take the time to clean out your compost pile completely and get it ready for the winter. Start by forking out all of the un-decomposed material on the top, and pile it to one side on a tarp or in a wheelbarrow. As you dig down, you'll finally come to the compost, and this should be saved in bags as mentioned before. It doesn't matter if your compost has bits and pieces of recognizable things still in it, as these will soon disappear once the compost is used.

When you've emptied the composter, you can start refilling it with the un-decomposed material that you removed from the top. You'll soon be cutting down your garden for the winter, and when you've done it you'll be able to continue adding layers of waste, activators, and minerals and start the whole process over again. It's a never-ending cycle, but at the end of each season you'll be left with a few bags of finished compost to use on your garden.

How should I use compost?

Your finished compost now contains a good blend of minerals and organic matter to improve the soil texture, as well as a natural source of nutrients for your plants. It also contains a wealth of soil-born life that keeps helping to create the soil solution or underground soup that feeds your plants.

So this black gold should be used where it will do the most good, and it should be treated as a very beneficial soil amendment. You can certainly spread it around everywhere in your garden, but it will be better for your plants if you use it in specific ways and in specific places.

Compost can be used to "top dress" individual annuals, perennials, shrubs and trees. This just means spreading it around the plant, over the root area, so it can become incorporated into the soil and its nutrients can work their way down to the roots.[fig. 12] If you do this on a regular basis during the spring and mid summer every season, you'll probably never need to use packaged fertilizer again.

You can also use compost anytime you're planting something. If you're putting new plants into the garden, or moving existing ones around, always add plenty of compost into the planting hole. Make the hole larger than is needed for the root ball, and fill it in with compost so that as new roots grow they will be moving into fertile soil for a long time. [Fig. 12]

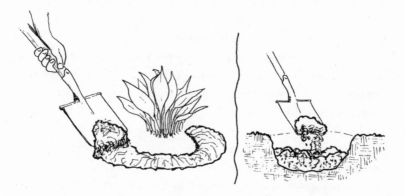

[FIG. 12] TOP DRESSING AND TRANSPLANTING WITH COMPOST

Compost is also a great addition to the soil mix in any of your containers, and can be anywhere from a quarter to a half of the mixture. It not only helps to retain moisture during the dry summer days, but it also helps to feed the plants in their frequently crowded conditions.

In the vegetable garden, you can add a thick layer of compost at the start of each season to be dug into the ground as you prepare it for planting. It's also useful for filling planting holes, and for a mid-season top dressing of larger vegetable plants like tomatoes and cabbages.

Large amounts of compost can also be used to improve soil problems at both ends of the spectrum. Light sandy soil that doesn't hold moisture for long will benefit from its water-retention properties. And heavy clay soil that drains slowly will be improved as the compost breaks up the fine particles into larger aggregates to improve drainage and aeration.

So depending on how much compost you are able to make, you should use it wherever it will benefit your most important plants or problem soils. You don't have to use all of it in the year that you make it, as compost can be kept sealed in bags for at least a couple of years. It may gradually lose some of its nitrogen content, but it will retain its other nutrients and will still be useful in improving the structure of your soil.

Can I compost during the winter?

With our cold temperatures during the winter, it's impossible to keep a composter going outside. The activity of the micro-organisms and any natural rotting is slowed to almost zero once it gets really cold.

I've heard of people setting up a compost box inside their garage during the winter, to keep its activity going in the warmth. The box had to be placed on a large waterproof tray to catch any liquid run-off, and as long as the pile stayed active with lots of air getting to the materials inside, it didn't smell.

That's not a solution that is convenient for everybody during the winter. So considering that most of your waste will be coming from the kitchen and not the garden, there is an alternative. Worms.

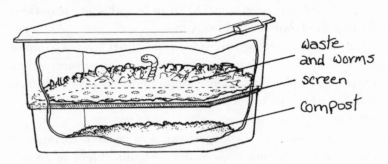

waste
and worms
screen
compost

[FIG. 13] VERMICOMPOSTING KIT

Vermicomposting, or composting using large numbers of worms, has become a quite reasonable alternative for Canada's winter months. The thought of having hundreds of live worms in the house is not always appealing to people, but before dismissing it out of hand you should understand how such a system works.

In principle, you start with a quantity of worms, usually "red wigglers" which are not the same as the ones we commonly find in the garden. You provide them with some bedding material, such as shredded newspaper, and then add moderate amounts of chopped up vegetable matter from your kitchen waste. The worms consume the waste and turn it into "worm castings," which look and smell like dark soil.

You can do this vermicomposting in a lidded plastic tub, usually about two feet long by a foot across. [fig. 13] It just needs a horizontal screen divider about a third of the way up to keep the waste and worms above, and let the finished castings fall through to the bottom.

There are kits available for vermicomposting, including a starter supply of the red wiggler worms. However, you'll never need to order the worms again because they multiply in their compost environment. When you've got a lot more worms than when you started, you can feed them more, start another composter or release them outside.

For those who are a bit squeamish about having worms in the home, there's really no need to worry about them getting loose and running all over your living room. Worms hate the light, and if you dump a bunch of them on a table, they will all cling together and try to stay in the dark. They will never venture outside the compost tub, even if you leave the lid off, so don't worry.

This sort of small indoor system will get rid of small quantities of food waste, about as much as is created by a two person family. If you create more waste, you could keep two or more vermicomposters going at once.

It's an interesting solution for anyone who feels badly about throwing away perfectly good vegetable waste during the winter.

THREE

Fertilizing

Why do I need to fertilize?

No matter how good your garden soil is, every year it needs some help to stay that way. Whether it's an early spring dose of fertilizer, or a major overhaul of the contents of the soil, there's always room for improvement.

One situation where conditions are always changing in the garden is the fertility of your soil. As plants grow they consume nutrients out of the soil, and the more plants you have and the bigger they grow, the more depletion there is. So you have to keep replenishing the soil in a busy section of garden with a steady supply of nutrients.

Some nutrients are more stable than others and they last a long time in the soil, whereas others are more volatile and disappear faster. Weather conditions can affect soil fertility, as lots of rain can flush certain nutrients away from the root area. The type of plants being grown also affects fertility, as different plants consume different quantities of the various soil nutrients.

So at the start of every growing season, and in some cases even during the season, your plants are going to need access to plenty of nutrients. It's up to you to make sure they're available.

In this book I refer to fertilizers in general, but right now I'll make my pitch for you to always use fertilizers that come from organic sources. Later in this chapter I'll explain the differences between "chemical" and "organic" fertilizers, and why I think the latter are better for your garden. I hope I can convince you to "go organic", mainly for the sake of your soil and the great long-term results that come from it.

What's in a fertilizer?

Plants consume lots of chemical elements during their growth. Some of them, such as carbon, are extracted from the air by the leaves. Most of the rest of the building blocks a plant needs are found in the soil, and are delivered to the plant through its system of feeder roots.

There are some elements, referred to as the macro-nutrients, which are needed in large quantities. There are secondary nutrients needed in smaller quantities, but which are equally important to proper growth. And finally there are the micro-nutrients that while essential, are needed only in trace amounts.

Macro-nutrients

Nitrogen (N) is the most important of these. It's responsible for all of the leaf and stem growth, which is the major part of the plant.

Phosphor (P) is next, helping to develop strong root systems, as well as flower and fruit growth.

Potassium (K) is the last of the major three nutrients, and it's mainly responsible for tissue strength, disease resistance and fruit development.

Secondary nutrients

Calcium and magnesium are freely available in ground limestone, sold for gardening as horticultural lime.

Sulphur, along with calcium and magnesium, is found in gypsum, but is also sold separately.

(Magnesium is also available at about 10% strength in Epsom Salt.)

Micro-nutrients

Very small, or "trace" amounts of boron, copper, iron, manganese and molybdenum are usually found naturally in any mineral soil, and need not be added separately.

Fertilizers sold in packages are by law labelled with the contents of the three macro nutrients, nitrogen (N), phosphor (P) and potassium (K) or N-P-K.

The numbers on the face of a fertilizer package refer to the percentages of actual N-P-K by weight in the fertilizer mix. [fig. 14] So a label saying 15-10-5 means that there is 15% nitrogen, 10% phosphor and 5% potassium in the package. The larger the numbers are, the stronger the concentration of active ingredients there are in the mix.

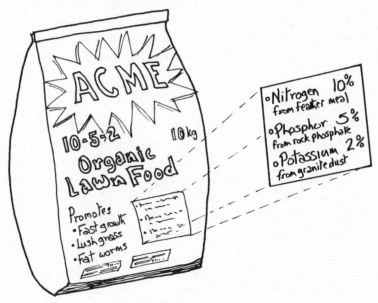

[FIG. 14] FERTILIZER LABEL

Since 15-10-5 only adds up to 30 percent of actual weight of active ingredients, you may wonder what's in the rest of the fertilizer. The balance in an artificial or "chemical" fertilizer is just the remaining elements used. For example, in sodium nitrate (NaNO3), only the nitrogen is reported, leaving the sodium and oxygen which weigh about seven times more. In an organic fertilizer, the balance is composed of inert or harmless ingredients that are similarly part of where the active ingredients came from.

They may not be listed on the package, but many fertilizers contain certain amounts of other useful elements such as calcium, sulphur and the trace elements.

Fertilizers are made with different ratios of the various chemical elements in them, and the reason for this is explained below.

Which of the many blends of fertilizer should I use?

Fertilizer manufacturers want you to succeed with their products, so they formulate them and identify them as carefully as possible. There will be blends that are suitable for lawns, trees, flowering plants, vegetables, tomatoes and roses, to name but a few. All of them will have slightly different formulae reflecting the major growth factors or important features of the plants in question.

However, the differences between them are in fact quite minor in most cases, and they are often very close to being the same thing. A fertilizer needed for tomatoes, for example, is quite similar to one needed for flowering perennials. With both of them we want lots of flowers and strong foliage growth.

In effect, many fertilizers are interchangeable in their uses. There are exceptions (as always). A lawn fertilizer should emphasise the nitrogen needed for leaf growth, so don't waste your money buying one that has high numbers for the P and K in the formula.

For the various types of plants that we grow in our gardens, here are some average fertilizer formulae. These numbers are just ratios, so the actual packages may have higher or lower numbers.

Flowering perennials, annuals & shrubs...... 5-7-3
Flowering vegetables (tomatoes, etc).......... 4-7-7
Green vegetables.................................... 7-2-2
Lawns.. 8-5-2
Hedges & trees....................................... 7-7-3

As well as the formula of the fertilizer, you'll find they are available in different formats, solid or liquid.

The solid fertilizers are usually granular so they can be spread easily. The most expensive ones should have each granule containing the exact ratio of all the nutrients in it. Less expensive blends will have all the ingredients granulated separately, and this is usually obvious by the different colours of the granules. In this case you should be careful to stir up the granules continually when you're applying them, so that there's a good chance of you distributing the correct ratio all over.

Solid fertilizers are designed to be what's called slow-release. They gradually break down in the soil over the course of a few weeks as they are exposed to moisture, and deliver their nutrients in a measured manner. They are most suitable for early spring application, sprinkled on the surface of the soil over the roots to be fed.

Liquid fertilizers are quite the opposite. They are designed to be mixed with water for application, and because of this they are available to the plant roots almost immediately. They are more suited to feeding containers and giving a late-season boost to large plants.

Water-soluble powders are another form of liquid fertilizer, as they are designed to only be used when diluted in water.

When should I apply fertilizer?

Fertilizers should only be used prior to a plant's growth period. Using them any other time is a waste of your money, and it could also end up being detrimental to the plants.

In the typical outdoor garden, a lot of growth happens in the spring as the ground warms up. Fertilizer should therefore be applied in the late winter or very early in the spring to take care of this growth spurt.

Grasses are often the first plants to wake up, so the lawn is one of the first places that should be fertilized. I'd even recommend that you get out on the lawn while the ground is still frozen hard and spread your fertilizer so that it can sink in during the early rains and be available right away. If you have to wait for the lawn to dry out before walking on it, you'll be feeding the lawn later than it would prefer.

Fertilizing your perennials and shrubs can wait until the ground has dried out and warmed up. These plants have food storage capacity in their root crowns that will take care of the very early growth.

Containers are often prepared quite early, so you should add an appropriate slow release fertilizer into the soil mixes you make for them.

As the spring progresses and you want to plant annuals in your flower beds and vegetables in your vegetable garden, these areas should be fertilized in the specific locations where plants are to be placed.

After your plants have been growing for a few weeks, you may want to consider some additional fertilizing to keep them strong. There are a few areas in your garden that will benefit from this.

Your lawn will have benefited from a very early spring feeding, but in late June you can apply a second amount of fertilizer to last it through the summer. Make sure that you water the lawn first, spread the fertilizer and then water it again to soak the granules down to the root area.

Containers with their limited size will soon be robbed of their nutrients, particularly if they are densely planted. Use a liquid fertilizer to feed them every two weeks starting around July.

And the vegetable garden is full of hungry plants, particularly the larger ones such as tomatoes and cabbages, and the ones that keep producing for a long time such as beans. These can always do with an application of the appropriate liquid fertilizer to keep their growth going at full speed.

Later in the season there's not much point in making any fertilizer applications, as the plants are slowing down their growth and getting ready to go dormant or die. In fact, feeding shrubs and hedges will only encourage weak late-season growth that will probably die during the winter months.

Besides, most of the rather volatile nitrogen in any fertilizer that you spread in the fall will have leached out of the soil by the spring, and you'll be wasting your money.

The only exception (remember them?) would be if you're seeding or laying sod for your lawn. If you apply a high phosphor fertilizer right away it will help a strong root system to develop before the winter.

How much fertilizer should I use?

Fertilizer applications must be done according to the manufacturer's directions. Each fertilizer formulation is made in a certain strength, and the application rate is decided based upon this. If you apply more than is recommended, there's a good chance that you could do some damage to the plants. In the case of fertilizers, more in NOT better.

This is much less of a problem if you're using organic fertilizers, as they are made from materials that are less toxic in large amounts and are slower to release their nutrients.

Which plants should I fertilize regularly?

All the plants in your garden should have access to a steady source of nutrients. However, different plants need access to these nutrients at different times during the season.

Spring bulbs grow each year thanks to the food they've stored from the year before in their bulbous stems. But as soon as their flower buds start to open they should be fed with a liquid fertilizer, to help them restore their energy for next year.

Perennials also have a small food supply stored in their stems and root crowns, to help get them started in the very early spring. But once they start growing lots of leaves and flower parts throughout the spring and summer, they will need to have nutrients available to their feeder roots.

Annuals start to grow in size as soon as they've been planted in the soil of your garden or a container, so they need access to lots of food right from the start. They may use up these nutrients quite quickly, particularly in the case of a container, so they will also need to be fed from mid-summer onwards every couple of weeks.

Vegetables are very similar to annuals, as they grow quickly in the spring. Crops like lettuce and peas need an immediate source of food, as they won't be around much in the summer. Larger plants like tomato, pepper, squash, chard and cabbage will need a steady supply from planting to harvest, so they may also need additional liquid feeding every two weeks from July onwards.

Lawns are one of the first things to show evidence of growth in the garden, so they should be fed as early as possible in the late winter or early spring. As mentioned above, you can even spread lawn fertilizer when there's still snow on the ground so that it's available as soon as the snow melts.

Shrubs, both the flowering and purely leafy types, are often neglected because people assume they are slow-growing and don't need much feeding. But in fact, these are large plants which produce a lot of foliage and stem growth in the early part of every season, and they can use up a lot of nutrients doing it. If the nutrient supply around the plant gets depleted, it sends out longer roots to search for more. But this can be a problem if there are lots of other plants in competition close to it, or if it's planted near buildings or pathways. There won't be enough food available, and the plant doesn't perform as well as it could. Every spring you should make sure your shrubs are fed.

Roses are particular perennial shrubs that need plenty of nutrients throughout the season. They should be fed in the early spring and again before each flush of blooms are expected. The addition of magnesium, in the form of Epsom Salt, strengthens the blooming cycle.

Trees are even larger versions of shrubs, with massive root systems spreading out around them. These roots do a very effective job of depleting the soil of nutrients, which is why other plants like grass and flowers don't do so well in competition with trees. They also tend to be neglected when it comes to regular feeding, but in a garden situation with lots of other plants around, they should be treated to a springtime dose of fertilizer.

How to apply fertilizer.
Slow-release granular fertilizer should be spread on the soil surface, before any mulching is done. The granules gradually dissolve as a result of moisture, and their components filter down into the soil solution where the roots can pick them up.

Plants absorb food from the newest "feeder" roots at the tips of their root systems, so that's where the fertilizer should

[FIG. 15] FEEDING AROUND PLANTS

be spread, not close to the stems. It should be applied in a circle around annuals, perennials and shrubs right over the outer root area of the plants.[fig. 15] If you can gently scratch the granules into the top inch of soil with a cultivator or rake without disturbing the roots, the granules will dissolve more effectively.

For garden beds containing annuals, perennials and shrubs, spread about a handful for every two feet of circle. So a small annual would need about one handful, a small perennial would probably need about two, and a shrub might require three or more handfuls.

Lawns need a nice even distribution of fertilizer to cover all the plants. The package will tell you how much a lawn of your area will need. If you've got a very small area of grass, you can spread by hand. For a larger area I'd recommend using a mechanical spreader, which whisks the granules in an even pattern as you walk back and forth. Either way, to make sure that you get even distribution you should divide the total amount of fertilizer in half. Spread one half walking up and down the lawn, and the other half walking left to right. I've also found for a small lawn it's very effective to spray with a liquid fertilizer through a hose-end applicator.

Trees are a bit different. The most efficient way to feed them is through a series of shallow holes over the root area.

First of all, measure out the amount of fertilizer needed. This should be based on the tree's size. Measure the diameter (width) of the trunk at four feet off the ground, and provide one kilo (two pounds) for every inch of diameter. Then walk out to the furthest spread of the tree's leaves, which is called the "drip line." All around the drip line, use a crowbar to punch a two inch wide hole about a foot deep at a spacing of every two feet. Count the number of holes, then divide the total amount of fertilizer into that many equal portions. Into each hole you pour a portion, followed by enough topsoil or compost to plug the hole.[fig. 16]

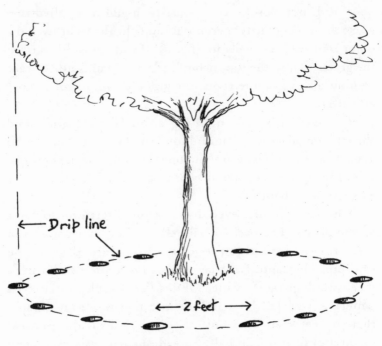

[FIG. 16]FEEDING A TREE

Fertilizing containers is also a bit different. I would recommend adding about one small handful for every plant you have in the container. Plant up everything in the soil mix, then spread the fertilizer evenly around the plants and lightly scratch it into the upper part of the soil.

Whenever you've applied granular fertilizer, it's a good idea to water the area immediately afterwards. This helps to settle the granules into the soil and it starts them dissolving right away.

Applying liquid fertilizer is a lot easier. Just mix it up in the recommended proportions in a watering can that has a "rose" or sprinkler head on the end. This will apply it more gently to the soil, and distribute it more evenly.

Water the root area away from the plant, not close to its stems, because that's where the feeder roots are spreading. And water the soil slowly, so that each area gets really soaked. Remember that the water has to have time to flow downwards and reach the level of the roots if it's to do any good. Just sprinkling the surface encourages the roots to grow upwards into shallow soil, and this can expose them to drying out much faster than if they are growing deeply.

What is foliar feeding?

Plants are not only able to ingest nutrients through their roots, but they can also absorb them in smaller amounts through their foliage. So if you spray the leaves of a plant with fertilized water, the plant is bound to benefit. This is not practiced on a large scale, because it's not economical, but for the home gardener it's quite feasible.

Just mix up a batch of fertilized water, put it in a sprayer and coat the upper surfaces of the leaves. In this way you can quickly give a plant a shot of extra nitrogen or phosphor at any time during the growing period.

This is a great use for "manure tea." To make a batch of manure tea, soak a small sack of manure in a bucket of water overnight. The resulting "tea" should be diluted half-and-half with water before applying to the foliage.

Why use organic rather than chemical fertilizers?

It's not so much a case of open warfare between two totally opposing camps. Most gardeners who have decided to use organic techniques just do their thing in their own way. And most other gardeners use chemical fertilizer because they figure it's easier and it produces good results.

I don't think the non-organic group, who are still in the majority, consciously go out of their way to avoid using organic techniques, any more than the average organically inclined gardener won't eat fruit or vegetables that have been grown using chemical fertilizers. It's hard to avoid them.

But now that municipal and provincial governments are

legislating in favour of organic pesticides, people are being forced to consider all sorts of organic alternatives in their gardening techniques. The next step after pesticides in going organic is learning how to provide the right soil fertility without relying on a bag of chemical fertilizer. But it's getting easier every season, and more and more people are trying it.

The most basic soil fertilizer that's available to a home gardener is compost. Whether you make it yourself or buy it ready-made in a bag, it's the essence of soil improvement. For more details on compost, see Chapter Two. But to have instant fertility in a bag, and still be organic, read on.

What's the difference between "chemical" and "organic" fertilizers?

Chemicals fertilizers work, and they do make plants grow. We've known for years that a plant doesn't really care whether the molecule of nitrogen that it consumes comes from ammonium nitrate, or from horse manure.

However, the soil cares. Over the long term, the mineral salts which chemical fertilizers are made from take a toll on the life in the soil. The plants are alive, but the soil isn't, and the idea behind organic husbandry is to improve the conditions that will encourage life and growth in the soil.

Chemical fertilizers provide the macro and secondary nutrients to the soil, but they use manufactured minerals to do it. This has a serious impact on the environment, mainly because of the amount of petrochemicals used to extract and purify them. The fertilizer granules break down quite quickly in the soil and give an immediate shot of nutrients to the plants, but have less long-term value. The mineral salts tend to make the soil more saline over time, making the soil less hospitable to living organisms, and we've all seen the damage that too much salt does to plants.

Organic fertilizers definitely do require some manu-facturing, but their sources are quite different. If you refer to the chart below, you can see the large-scale sources of the common elements used in organic fertilizer manufacturing. These sources are often the wastes or by-products of some other processing which would otherwise become garbage. Once processed and granulated into a fertilizer, these products break down gradually in the soil and add measured amounts of nutrients over a good part of the growing season.

So the biggest argument against chemical fertilizers and in favour of using organic source fertilizers is in the long term impact they have on the organisms in the soil. By encouraging soil life, organic techniques build a healthy soil which in turn produces healthy plants.

⟋ ORGANIC SOURCES OF NUTRIENTS ⟍

Alfalfa meal (nitrogen)
Blood meal (nitrogen)
Bone meal (phosphor)
Cottonseed meal (nitrogen)
Crab meal (nitrogen)
Egg shells (calcium)
Feather meal (nitrogen)
Fish meal (nitrogen)
Fish bone meal (phosphor)
Granite dust (potassium)
Gypsum (calcium, sulphur)
Hoof meal (nitrogen)
Kelp (potassium)
Limestone (calcium, magnesium)
Manures (nitrogen, phosphor)
Rock phosphate (phosphor)
Shrimp meal (nitrogen)
Soybean meal (nitrogen)
Wood ash (potassium)

How are organic fertilizers packaged and sold?

Organic fertilizers used to be quite difficult to find for sale, and also tricky to use. A few adventurous garden centres sold packages of bat guano with hand-written instructions on how to use it.

But today, organic fertilizers are big business. The demand by gardeners for organic products has spurred the growth of a new segment of the industry. The same manufacturers who package chemical fertilizers now also sell organic ones, and there are a few successful companies that specialize in organics only.

The typical granular slow-release organic fertilizer is now sold in the same way as the chemical ones always were. They are pre-formulated for specific tasks, such as lawns or flowers. There are small one and two kilo packages for small jobs, and there are larger five and ten kilo bags for larger applications. The granules are easy to handle, can be distributed using mechanical spreaders, and don't have any disagreeable odours.

You can also buy packages of individual ingredients such as bone meal, blood meal or superphosphate to add specific nutrients to your garden soil or compost pile.

Organic fertilizers come in water-soluble formats too, usually thick consistency liquids which require mixing with water in a watering can or through a hose-end applicator. They are very economical sources of nutrients, particularly useful for mid-season feeding. Some of these have a faintly oceanic smell, reflecting their sources, but it's not at all unpleasant.

You can also feed your garden with packaged composts and manures, which because of their inherent nutritive value have to carry the mandatory N-P-K fertilizer labels. The values of the nutrients in these products are usually quite low, in the range of 1-0.5-0.5, but they are no less useful because of it. The animal and vegetable raw materials have gone through a commercial decomposing process, which produces an agreeable–smelling product that is difficult to distinguish from good soil. If you can't get hold of real farm manures or make your own compost, these are excellent alternatives.

Testing organic versus chemical results.
The true test of the efficiency of any theory or product is to put it through a controlled test, preferably one with some scientific standards behind it. The chemical versus organic approach to gardening is a theory which needed this sort of comparison.

A few years ago, a professor of soil science at the Nova Scotia Agricultural College by the name of Phil Warman published the results of a test he's been running for 12 years. He wanted to know which would produce better vegetable yields, a garden using strictly compost or one using chemical fertilizers.

In his test he grew an identical selection of vegetables in two different gardens over that time, one using compost and the other using chemical fertilizer. The packaged fertilizers were regular varieties bought at local stores, and his compost was made from garden and kitchen waste along with some straw and manure.

His results really show the benefit of doing experiments over the long term, and not just jumping to quick conclusions.

For the first couple of years, Warman found the yields from the chemically fertilized crops were higher. They performed the way the manufacturers promised they would in the TV ads, producing big lush plants. But by the fifth year, the results from the composted garden were improving and the other garden was slowing, and the two of them had equal crop yields.

And from then on, the composted garden out-produced the other one. This was even more noticeable when the gardens were under conditions of stress from things like dry spells or insect infestations. The composted garden continued its high yields, and the other one didn't.

By analyzing the soils and the plants, Warman was able to explain why it happened this way. He found the components in the compost were traditionally slower to release their nutrients to the soil, whereas vegetables have a short growing period. So in the first couple of years the plants in the composted garden didn't get as many nutrients as they needed. But over time the compost mineralized, the nutrients became constantly available, and the plants got all they wanted.

On a purely nutritional level, the professor found no difference at all between the two groups of vegetables. All the vitamins and nutritional elements were identical from the two gardens.

Warman's advice is to go with compost in your garden, but you have to be prepared to stick with it if you want to see the results over the long term.

How can a fungus help soil fertility?

There are certain beneficial fungi that occur naturally in the soil that can vastly improve a plant's ability to grow. These mycorrhizal fungi form a symbiotic relationship with the roots of the plant, setting up a network of thread-like fungus growth which almost doubles the effective nutrient gathering ability of the plant's own roots. With a larger effective root system, a plant can increase its growth noticeably. [fig. 17]

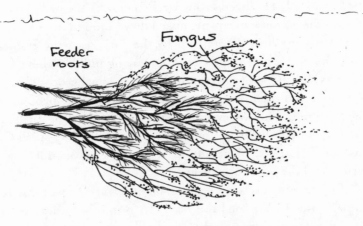

[FIG. 17] FUNGUS AND ROOTS

The horticulture industry has taken note of this phenomenon, and has responded with a series of products that can introduce the appropriate fungus into the soil around a plant.

The first of these products on the market are sold under the name MYKE, and are separately formulated for flowers, vegetables and shrubs. The fungus spores are mixed together with an inert peat-like powder, which has to be introduced at planting time so that it's actually touching the plant's roots. The spores are activated in the presence of moisture and the host plant, and once they spread it's like having a whole extra set of roots working for the plant. The plant has an increased growth rate, and as an added bonus the fungi make the plant less susceptible to soil-born diseases.

I've used it in trials with shrubs and perennials, and the comparative results that I've had in my own garden are quite noticeable.

FOUR

Watering & Irrigation

Water is the most essential ingredient for plant growth. Plants will grow in poor soil, under hostile weather conditions and even with insufficient light. But if you deny a plant water it will surely die, no matter how good the remaining conditions are.

Conversely, if you provide consistently moist conditions for plants, they will reward you with reliable and even spectacular growth.

We rely upon the weather a great deal to provide the majority of the water needs of our gardens, but nature is not always cooperative. Many times, it's up to us to make sure that our plants get the right amount of moisture to grow properly.

What affects how much moisture there is in the soil?

There are three main factors that affect how much moisture your soil holds. The type of soil, the amount of plant activity and the effects of weather. Let's deal with them in order.

The *soil type* is critical to how water enters, passes through and is retained in the soil.

Starting with the worst case scenario, consider a heavy clay soil. Its tightly-packed particles resist the entry of water and force it to rest on the surface for long periods of time, where it can run off or be lost to evaporation. Clay also slows the passage of water downwards, with the same results. The only good thing about a heavy clay soil is its ability to retain moisture. But this is offset by the fact that it discourages extensive root growth, and it can hold too much water for too long a time which leads to roots being cut off from their air supply.

On the other end of the soil spectrum, a very sandy soil also has problems. The large sand particles allow the penetration and passage of water through its gaps alright, but their inability to hold water on their surfaces results in a soil which drains almost immediately. [fig. 18] The very fine feeder roots dry out and die unless the plants have developed some drought-tolerance.

The ideal soil (as discussed in Chapter One) is one which has a blend of different-sized particles. A mixture of clay, silt and sand along with some organic matter helps to form aggregates that collectively have the best properties of all of them individually.

This synergy gives a soil that drains well through its many gaps, but which is also able to hold a certain amount of moisture on its various-shaped surfaces. And the presence of organic matter, which breaks down into the gummy liquid called humus, provides water retention through its sponge-like ability to hold water.

Plant density also affects how much water stays in the soil. In the typical landscaped home garden there's usually an abundance

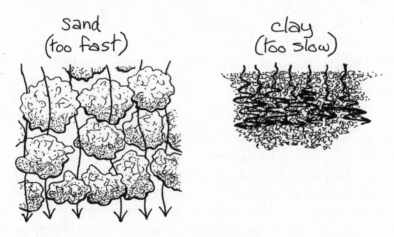

[FIG. 18] SOIL TYPES VS WATER RETENTION

of plants, all located quite close to each other. We have a tendency to abhor empty spaces, so we plant everywhere that there's the least open soil. Shrubs are cheek-by-jowl with annual and perennial flowers, often with large trees nearby and with a lawn surrounding it all. This means that underground there's quite a competition for root space, for nutrition, and for water.[fig. 19]

So any water that enters the soil of our crowded gardens tends to get used by the upper-level feeder root systems of the plants. It takes a considerable amount of water to be able to penetrate to the lower depths of the soil structure. And plants with a lot of surface roots encouraged by light waterings will suffer much sooner under drought conditions than those with deep roots to draw moisture from lower areas.

[FIG. 19] TYPICAL ROOT DENSITY IN A GARDEN

Finally, the *weather*. The rain, sun, wind and ambient temperature all play a key role in the amount of moisture held in the soil.

As a natural source of water, rainfall is of course critical to how much moisture is delivered to the soil. But how it rains is important too. A heavy summer deluge delivers a lot of water in a short period of time, sometimes too much for the ability of the soil to quickly absorb it, and the result is soil erosion or even damage to shallow-rooted plants. A thick layer of mulch, as discussed in Chapter One, can save some of this erosion from happening. The ideal rainfall is a gentle one that lasts for a long time. It may not be good picnic weather, but it's

70

great for the garden.

The wind is an enemy of soil moisture for two reasons. It sucks the moisture from the surface of any exposed soil by evaporation. And it blows away the moisture given off or "transpired" by the leaves of a plant, forcing it to suck up and transpire some more. The combined effects of this "evapo-transpiration" can exhaust the moisture supply around a plant quite quickly. Again, mulch is an effective barrier against this problem.

Sunshine, much as we love it in the summer, is also an enemy of moisture in the soil. The strong mid-summer rays of the sun are like a heater drying out the surface of the soil. They also heat the surface of leaves, forcing the plant to rush more moisture to cool the leaves down. More "evapotranspir-ation".

All of these previous weather effects also combine to create a specific ambient temperature, and if these temperatures are high they also become a problem to the garden. We might love the freedoms that warm temperatures bring, but unfortunately there's a price to pay in soil moisture. Warmth means more plant transpiration, makes surface evaporation more intense, and absorbs more moisture into the air molecules from wher-ever it can get it. And even if high humidity in the air does reduce the transpiration rate of plants, it also unfortunately slows the growth rate of the plants.

How much water does the garden need?

Whether the garden gets it moisture from the rain or from your watering efforts, there's definitely an optimum supply needed by the various individual plants in order to grow properly. If they get more, they may react by growing better. If they get a bit less you may see a slowdown in growth.

There are definite differences in the water needs of dif-ferent plants. Some are classified as drought-resistant, some are drought-tolerant, and others drought-intolerant. If you want to reduce the water requirements of your garden, referred to as *xeriscaping*, you could use plants from grassland and desert regions, such as *achillea, anthemis, aster, coreopsis, echinacea, helianthus, kochia, liatris, mirabilis, portulaca and rudbeckia*. Others, such as *iris, lythrum, lobelia and monarda* are so drought-intolerant they only thrive in soggy conditions.

However, some generalizations are needed when considering the moisture needs of your own garden. Unless you've deliberately planted drought-resistant varieties, the following are guidelines for the water needs of most of the plants in your garden. If nature doesn't provide sufficient water, it will be up to you to do so.

Flowers (both annuals and perennials)
- two inches a week.
Shallow-rooted vegetables (leaf crops, root crops)
-three inches a week.
Deep-rooted large vegetables (tomato, cabbage, beans, squash) – two inches a week.
Trees & shrubs – two inches a week.
Lawns – one inch a week.

You can measure the weekly amount of rain with a simple rainfall meter. It catches the rain drops and feeds them into a marked measuring tube.

You can create your own with a coffee can placed under the open sky. Measure the collected rainfall each week. You can use a ruler as a dipstick, or mark the inside of the can with a waterproof pen.

What's the best way to water a flower or vegetable garden?
The easy answer to this question is "deeply." Water in the soil is only useful if gravity can pull it down through the various levels, past the roots, leaving behind small amounts on each soil aggregate. It takes quite a bit of water to achieve this "field

capacity" of almost saturation in a well-drained soil.

When you're doing the watering yourself, there's absolutely no point in applying too little water. If all you do is a quick sprinkle with a hose, you'll do more damage than good. The water will remain near the surface, where it can be lost to evaporation. It will encourage new roots to head upwards to it, exposing them to the most fragile surface region of the soil. And you'll create "wet and dry" cycles of moisture in the soil, which can cause flowers and fruit (such as tomatoes) to expand too quickly and split.

The ideal is to aim for a consistent level of moisture in the soil. All of the plants in your garden will respond to this with a consistent and steady rate of growth. This means never letting your soil dry out too much if nature doesn't supply rain, and it means mulching the soil surface to trap the moisture underneath once it's there.

As far as watering techniques go, there are a few to avoid and a few that are good.

Don't use a sprinkler to water your garden. They are for the lawn. Water sprayed in the air will evaporate, and it's been estimated that you can lose up to 80 percent of the water from a sprinkler due to this. You also waste water by spraying the foliage of the plants and not the roots, and spraying water onto flowers and leaves can encourage disease.

Don't use a hose with a focusable nozzle on the end to water your garden. If you have it dialed to a thin stream you'll gouge the soil with it. If you have it dialed to a finer spray, you'll get it all over the foliage (see above).

Do use a wand with a "rose" on the end of your hose. The rose splits the power of the water stream into many smaller more gentle individual sprays with less pressure behind them.[fig. 20] They cause less damage to the foliage, less disturbance to the soil and the small streams of water are more easily absorbed into the surface. When using a hose with a wand, place it low down under the foliage near the soil and spray just around the roots of the plants. Be patient, keep the water pressure turned down so that it's a slower application which can be easily absorbed into the soil and then apply plenty to each area.

Do use a soaker hose which applies a small amount of water over a long period of time. You can buy several types, some with small holes punched their length and others which are made of porous materials and "weep" small amounts of water into the soil. They can be laid on the surface or buried an inch or two under the soil, and should be laid so they snake their way along the centre section of each bed.

[FIG. 20] WAND AND ROSE SPRAYER

Do water slowly and for a long time, whichever way you chose to do it. Remember, "deeply" is key to watering properly. Roots are attracted by water, so the deeper the water is able to penetrate, the deeper the roots will grow. Deeper roots mean a plant that's anchored better, and which is better able to withstand the occasional dry spells by drawing moisture up from the depths.

What's the best way to water a lawn?

For a small lawn the sprinkler is still the favored method for spreading large amounts of water over a wide area.

There are three main types that can be attached to the end

of a garden hose. The oscillating type swings back and forth covering a roughly rectangular area. The rotating style spins water out in a circular pattern. And the adjustable-head spray usually has half-a-dozen different spray patterns, from long narrow rectangles to large squares.[fig. 21]

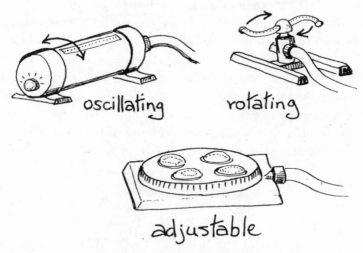

oscillating   rotating

adjustable

[FIG. 21] LAWN SPRINKLER TYPES

There are other variations on these patterns, such as those that crawl along the lawn, those with ring-shaped sprayers and others like short poles stuck in the lawn to give some height to the spray. Which one you use depends on the size and shape of your lawn.

However, no matter which delivery system you use, remember the water has to penetrate deeply. Lawns are no different from shrubs or perennials. They too can be coaxed into growing remarkably deep roots if the water attracts them downwards instead of just towards the surface. The deeper the roots, the more able your lawn will be to resist the effects of dry spells when watering restrictions are often applied by municipal authorities.

Leave your sprinkler running until you've applied one inch of water to the lawn. To easily measure this, place an empty tuna can on the lawn under the main part of the water spray. When it's full, you've sprayed one inch of water.

For larger lawns which mean hauling the hose and sprinkler around to different locations every time you want to water it, you should consider installing an in-ground sprinkler system. (See later in this chapter under "irrigation systems.")

In Chapter Three when talking about fertilizing I made reference to using a hose-end applicator to both water and feed a lawn. This particular gadget looks like a jam jar with a nozzle attached to its lid. You fill the jar with some concentrated liquid fertilizer, attach it to the lid and then screw your water hose into the open end of the nozzle. When the water is turned on, a venturi effect sucks a measured amount of fertilizer into the water stream coming out of the nozzle. [fig. 22]

[FIG. 22] HOSE-END APPLICATOR

It's a handy way to spread a water-soluble fertilizer while watering. I find it useful for giving the lawn a shot of fertilizer even before the snow has melted, or for when the lawn is too soggy to walk on in the late winter. It's also handy for a mid-season fertilizer application to the flower or vegetable garden, but you have to be careful not to spray it all over the foliage. Aim low, and try to gently spray only the soil surface.

When is the best time to water?
There has been some disagreement in horticultural writing as

to the best time to water a garden. Is it the morning, the evening, both or neither?

One thing that nearly all agree upon is that it's good to water in the early part of the day. This gives the plants a ready supply of moisture in the soil before they start their most active period of daily growth, when light spurs them into a busy period of photosynthesis. It also provides their roots with plenty of water to face the hottest part of the day, when they lose the most moisture by transpiring through their leaves. So that's a couple of major reasons for watering as early as possible in the morning, even before the sun rises.

As for watering in the evening, I've seen arguments in favour of not letting the soil stay dry overnight after a hot dry daytime. But those were recommendations applying mainly to large-scale growing applications, not the home garden. I've also heard the old adage that "plants don't like to go to bed with their feet wet," which may be classed as unscientific gardener's lore, but which had some reason to be said in the first place.

My recommendation would be to try and keep your watering times mostly to the very early part of the day, for all of the reasons mentioned above. But if your schedule only gives you time in the late afternoon or evening to water on a very dry day, then do it when you can.

Either way, it's best to water when the air temperature is low, so that the water has a chance to penetrate into the soil before a lot of it gets lost to evaporation.

Why do containers need so much watering?
Any container, from the smallest window box to the largest planter, only has a finite amount of soil in it. And that soil can only contain a finite amount of water. So containers have a strike against them right from the start.

We know they're going to need watering much more often than the soil in the garden, with its huge reservoir of potential moisture and with the deep roots of plants to go after it.

Containers are also much more exposed to the evaporation threats of sun and wind, particularly if they're made of porous materials such as terracotta or materials such as metal, which heat up quickly. And we put lots of plants in them to make them look full and lush, which creates a big moisture competition among the roots.

So you have to get used to the idea of your containers needing water more frequently than your garden. It may be a couple of times a week in the cooler periods up to twice a day during the hottest driest part of the summer.

[23] CACHE POT INSIDE CLAY POT

However, you can minimize the watering requirements of your containers by affecting some of the causes of them drying out.

Use large deep pots, window boxes and planters. They contain more soil, and therefore a larger reservoir of water. Depth is the best way to add more volume.

Use mulch on the exposed soil surfaces of all your containers, even small pots. It's amazing how much this reduces water loss.

Clay pots evaporate water very quickly, but they do look nice. You can put your plants in a plastic pot *inside* the decorative clay one. [fig. 23] For large clay pots you can line the inside with a plastic sheet before you fill it with soil mix. Better yet, at the beginning of each season paint a waterproof wood sealer on the inside of the clay pot and let it dry completely before planting.

There are an increasing number of containers for sale with built-in water reservoirs. They allow the soil mix to absorb a measured amount of water, and keep it moist over a longer period of time. All you have to do is keep the reservoir filled.

There are many other new materials being used for containers that are not porous and that hold water very well.

Your soil mix can also be improved to hold more water. I'm impressed with the performance of the new clear plastic polymer crystals that swell and absorb up to 400 times their weight in water. They're sold under various names such as "Soil Moist" or "Water Crystals." You only need half a teaspoon of crystals mixed into the soil of an eight inch pot to keep absorbing and giving back moisture for a whole season. Also you can replace the peat in your soil mix with coir fibres, taken from the inside of coconut shells. It absorbs and gives back water faster than peat, and has a neutral pH. You can also add vermiculite to the soil mix for containers, as it also absorbs plenty of moisture.

My favourite container soil mix is as follows:
Two parts potting soil
Two parts compost
One part perlite (for drainage)
One part vermiculite
One part coir

For a lighter-weight hanging container mix:
One part potting soil
One part compost
One part vermiculite
Two parts coir

How useful are irrigation systems?

A good irrigation system takes much of the work out of watering a garden, particularly a large one. It can look after your lawn, your planting beds and even your containers. You can hook the system to timers so that it will operate without your intervention, which is particularly useful if you spend time away in the summer.

The only drawback is the cost of installing an irrigation system. For a small property that can be fed from one or two water taps, there are quite inexpensive do-it-yourself systems available. For a larger property you'll have to consider a dedicated system that should be installed by professionals. However, the principles behind both types of systems are the same.

Lawns are usually watered from locations around the edges by angled sprayers and from the centre by rotating sprayers. They can form overlapping sprays of water to cover the whole lawn, no matter what shape it is.

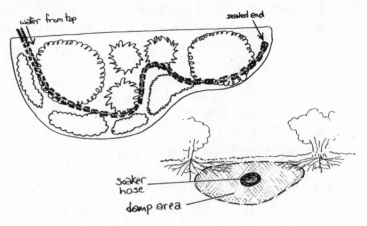

[FIG. 24]SOAKER HOSE

Flower and vegetable beds are best watered with either soaker hoses or microsprays. Soaker hoses use flexible porous lines either on the surface or just below it to weep a band of moisture into a bed.[fig. 24] Microsprays are small spray heads positioned just above the soil surface that direct a fine mist over a few square feet, so you need a series of them to cover a whole bed.[fig. 26]

Individual shrubs or trees are usually watered from drip systems. These are thin tubes fed from a main water line, leading directly to the plant. They drip a measured amount of water to one spot, so several of them may be needed for a large plant.

Containers can be watered using a variation of the drip system. On the end of the tube is an adjustable "dribbler" that slowly drips a low amount of water into the container over a long period of time.

Systems covering a large garden require some professional help in planning, along with the equipment to lay the high-pressure in-ground pipes and hook up all the delivery points.[fig. 25] They should also use state-of-the-art computer controlled timers to regulate the watering at different points throughout the system.

Small-scale low-pressure systems can be bought off-the-shelf through stores or catalogues. They are quite inexpensive and thanks to modern materials are quite efficient, although they are designed to work for garden beds and containers rather than lawns. You need to plan a layout to feed the system's various spray heads and drippers, and then install them quite permanently. These small systems can also be controlled by in-line timers, so you don't have to get up early in the morning to run them.

The larger high-pressure systems are less prone to clogging over time than the smaller ones, depending on the mineral deposits in your water. But they can be cleaned out with an application of vinegar and water.

If you want to save yourself a lot of time and also assure yourself of great growth, an irrigation system of some sort is a very good investment.

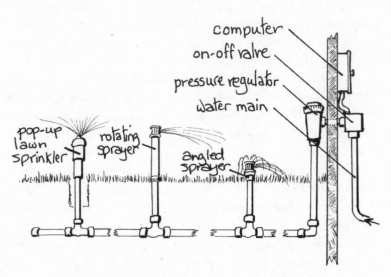

computer
on-off valve
pressure regulator
water main

pop-up
lawn
sprinkler

rotating
sprayer

angled
sprayer

[FIG. 25] HIGH-PRESSURE IRRIGATION SYSTEM

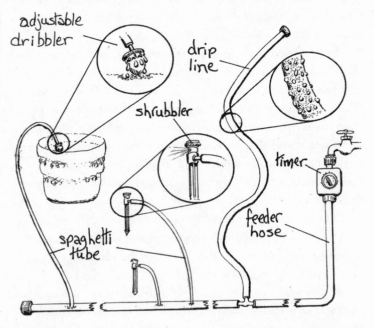

adjustable
dribbler

drip
line

shrubbler

timer

spaghetti
tube

feeder
hose

[FIG. 26] LOW-PRESSURE IRRIGATION SYSTEM AND MICROSPRAYERS

Xeriscaping.

A style of gardening that uses drought-tolerant plants is called "xeriscaping."

This term has been used to describe the landscaping techniques developed in the hot southern desert regions of the United States. Natural water supplies are very limited there, and to avoid relying on elaborate irrigation systems and using up precious water resources, a school of landscaping came about that relies on the tolerance of plants to withstand prolonged dry conditions, as well as moisture-trapping and heat avoidance techniques.

In our northern climate we generally don't have quite the same desert conditions to contend with, although there are some prairie and western regions which certainly face extended dry periods every year.

But there are definitely things we can learn from these xeriscaping techniques about minimizing the use and waste of water, and about planting varieties that are less demanding of water.

There are many varieties of flowering annuals, perennials and shrubs that are familiar to northern gardeners that are also quite drought-tolerant. There are the obvious ones such as most ornamental grasses and the succulents like *sedum spectabile*. But there are plenty of others such as *achillea*, *liatris*, *salvia* and *rudbeckia* that don't need as much water as we perhaps give them.

If you're concerned about water consumption in your decorative garden, and want to focus more of your selection on drought-tolerant plants, I suggest you refer to books such as *Dryland Gardening* by Canadian author Jennifer Bennett.

FIVE

Planting

Looking after and maintaining a garden can be quite a daunting task, one which we'll try to simplify in Chapter 10.

But when it comes to actually putting plants into the ground or moving them around, more fear seems to be generated in the minds of gardeners than with perhaps any other job.

I hope to show you that this fear is unnecessary, and that planting and messing around with plants can be the most rewarding part of gardening.

It's where you really get to touch things. You feel the details in the structure of the soil, you become quite intimate with the parts of plants that are normally hidden from view and you gain confidence in handling plants in the various stages of their life.

There can be failures, but more often you have the satisfaction of seeing things that you nurtured come to fruition.

One word of warning. Whenever you're doing any planting or transplanting, try to do it on a cloudy day. That may sound a bit unreasonable, but plants are bound to be disturbed during even the most careful planting procedure. The last thing they need is to be subjected to a hot sunny day where they're forced to transpire moisture at a heavy rate through a root system that's just been completely disrupted. They'll often react by wilting, and no amount of watering will fix the problem. If you can't avoid a sunny day, provide some shade to the newly-planted plants. Set up a cloth, cardboard or wood screen to keep the direct sun off them for the day.[fig. 27]

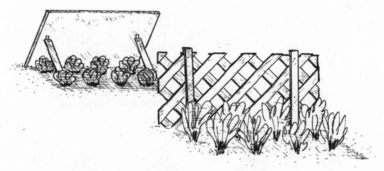

[FIG. 27] PROVIDING TEMPORARY SHADE

When and how do you plant spring bulbs?

Spring bulbs are completely hardy through our below-freezing winters, so we plant them in the fall of the year and let them over-winter underground to bloom in the very early spring.

In fact, most of the spring bulbs we grow actually require some time exposed to very cold temperatures in order to break their dormancy and start growing.

When we buy a spring bulbs for planting in the fall, they are completely ready to start their growth. The bulb, which is really a swollen part of the stem, is in fact a storage organ that contains all the energy needed to grow a full plant with leaves and flowers. All we have to do is give it the right home.

Spring bulbs need a few weeks of being in the soil to grow a set of roots before they start to grow leaves or flower stems. The longer they get to grow before the ground freezes, the better their root system will be, and the stronger they'll be next spring. It's also a lot easier to plant bulbs before the weather turns really cold and miserable. So it's good idea to get them into the ground in the early fall, well before winter freezes the soil. [fig. 28]

The planting depth is the most important aspect, because if they're too deep or too shallow, they won't perform properly. The larger bulbs such as tulip, daffodil, hyacinth and allium should be planted so their bases are seven inches below the

85

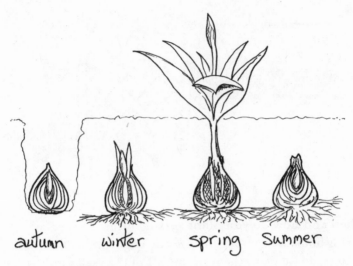

autumn   winter   spring   Summer

[FIG. 28] BULB GROWTH CYCLE

surface. The smaller bulbs such as crocus, scilla, galanthus, small narcissus, chionodoxa, and small iris should have their bases five inches below the surface.

Once you know the depth to plant, it's just a matter of deciding how you're going to spread out the bulbs. There are a couple of popular methods, either in clumps or randomized. By planting in clumps, you benefit from the impact of having a group of blooms all in one place making a nice display. Randomizing is fun to do with smaller bulbs in a lawn or an area with ground cover.

To plant in a clump, dig out an oval or triangular shaped hole about ten inches deep. It should be large enough so that all the bulbs can fit in it with about two inches between them. Mix the removed soil with some compost, and then refill the hole with the mixture until you've reached either the seven inch or the five inch level, depending on which type of bulb you're planting. If the soil is very heavy with clay, provide better drainage by putting a one inch layer of sand under the base of each bulb. At this time you can also spread the recommended amount of mycorrhizal fungus on the soil.

Place the bulbs in the hole, pointed end up, with a couple of inches between them. Press them firmly into the soil, and then fill in around them with the rest of the removed soil. Gently press the soil into place, and then soak the whole area with water, as it's the moisture that will start the bulbs growing their roots.

To plant in a random pattern, it's best to take a handful of bulbs and toss them casually on the ground, and then plant them exactly where they land. This will give you a more random pattern than if you try to plant them deliberately. Rather than digging one large hole for random planting, you'll have to use

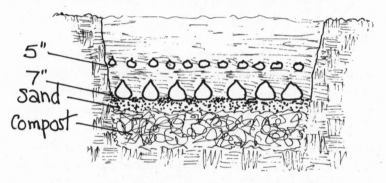

[FIG. 29] PLANTING SPRING BULB COMBINATIONS

a stick or a narrow trowel to make a five or seven inch deep hole. Drop the bulb into the hole, making sure the pointed end stays upright, and fill in on top of it with some topsoil. Then water the whole area thoroughly to get the bulbs growing.

When the ground has frozen, spread some mulch to keep the bulbs in place throughout the winter.

If your planting space is limited, there's one trick you can do when planting spring bulbs in clumps to get a succession of blooms in the same place. [fig. 29] Once you've planted some larger bulbs at the seven inch depth, fill in a couple of inches of soil and then put in some smaller bulbs at the five inch level. You can do this with combinations like crocuses and tulips, or scilla and daffodils. That way the smaller bulbs will bloom first, and the larger bulbs will push up past them to bloom later. You'll have a double showing in the same amount of space.

How do you care for your bulbs in the spring?

As mentioned, when you plant spring bulbs they contain all the energy they need to grow into beautiful flowers. But if you want them to come back next year you have to help them along a bit in the early spring. If you were to dig up a tulip, for example, right after it bloomed you would find that the bulb was quite soft and empty feeling. This is because all the flesh has been used up providing the energy to grow the leaves and stems and flowers you've just appreciated. Your job is to help the bulb replenish that energy.

In the early spring, as soon as you see a flower stem growing up through the leaves of a spring bulb, it's time to feed the bulb. This is more important with the larger bulbs like tulip and daffodil, but the smaller ones like crocus also benefit from it.

Just mix a general-purpose fertilizer in your watering can and really soak the area where the bulbs are growing. You can even do it twice, to make sure the nutrient-laden water gets down to the root area.

Then, when the flower has finished blooming nicely and it's starting to fade, snap it off the top of the stem to prevent the flower from going to seed. Making seeds takes energy away from the underground replenishment process, and we want the plant to focus all its energy on renewal.

Allow the leaves to keep growing and gathering energy into the bulb. Don't tie them in a knot as this will interfere with the flow of sap. After a couple of weeks the plants will show you when this "ripening" process has finished when their leaves gradually turn yellow and then brown. As soon as this happens you can cut the foliage off at ground level and forget about the bulbs until next spring.

If waiting for the leaves to ripen is an eyesore for you, or

they get in the way of other planting you want to do, then you'll
have to remove the bulbs before they ripen. Use a spade to dig
them up, with lots of soil still attached around the roots. Place
each clump on its side somewhere out of the way, such as under
a hedge, lay the leaves on the ground and allow them to ripen.
Then you can shake off the excess soil, dry them out indoors,
cut off the foliage and store the bulbs somewhere cool and dry
for planting next fall.

Tulip and hyacinth bulbs will come back for you for a couple
of years before they stop producing. Large narcissus bulbs
(daffodils) will stay strong for a few more years, and the small
bulbs will last much longer. When you see a reduction in the
number of flowers coming up, dig up the bulbs and break off
all the little bulblets from the base of each one. You can replant
the original bulbs as long as they are plump and the same size
as when you bought them. Unless you have the patience to wait
several years for them to get larger, I would throw away the
small bulblets rather than planting them.

When and how do you plant summer bulbs?

There's a group of plants that can last in your garden for years,
but which at the same time aren't hardy enough to be able to
stay in the ground over the winter.

We call them summer "bulbs" to make it simpler, but in
actual fact they're a collection of tubers, corms and rhizomes.
They are varieties such as tuberous begonia, caladium, dahlia,
freesia, gladiolus, canna and calla lily. They can all keep
performing well for many years, but because of their sensitivity
to cold they have to be lifted out of the ground in the fall and
stored indoors.

The key to success with summer bulbs is to plant them when
it's warm enough, and not before. They don't react well to being
stuck in cold ground. By planting them too early in an attempt
to get a head start, they will start off slowly and won't develop a
good root system. A soil thermometer, some of which look the

same as the ones you stick into a roast in the oven, should read 16 degrees C (61F) to be safe. This may mean waiting until late May or even June before planting these bulbs, but rushing will only delay things later.

Starting summer bulbs indoors early.
You can buy these summer bulbs in the early spring, and you can even plant some of them then, but it has to be done indoors. This gives them a head start on the season, and you may also get a much larger plant with the possibility of more flowers than one planted later. The best bulbs to start early indoors are those of begonia, caladium and dahlia.

Planting these varieties early indoors requires some pots and the potting soil to fill them. The pots should be a minimum of eight inches (20cm) wide. This will allow you to plant one large dahlia tuber or about four begonia tubers.

* For begonias and caladiums fill the pot three-quarters full of potting soil, position the tubers spaced evenly apart with the rough side down, and add more soil until they are half buried.

For dahlias just half-fill the pot with soil, and position the tuber at a 45 degree angle, with the stem end up and the pointed end down. Fill in around the tuber so that it remains at an angle, and bury it as much as possible.[fig. 30]

All the pots should be dunked into a tray of water for about ten minutes to absorb as much moisture as they can from the bottom, then allow them to drain. They should be placed either under fluorescent lights or where they will get as much light as possible. After a week or two you'll see a green stems sprouting from the tubers, which will produce leaves and grow towards the light.

Keep the lower part of the soil moist and keep turning the pot so that the stems don't grow crooked, until the season warms up enough for them to be transplanted outdoors, as described later.

dahlia

caladium
or
begonia

[FIG. 30] STARTING SUMMER BULBS IN POTS

Planting summer bulbs outdoors.

Once the weather and the soil have warmed up enough for them to be planted, the plants you started early and the other bulbs you purchased deserve the very best of soil conditions in which to grow for the season.

For all of your tuberous begonia, caladium, dahlia, freesia, gladiolus, canna and calla lily bulbs or plants, make sure you prepare their planting bed very carefully. All of them like soil that drains really well, because bulbous plants are not suited to soggy clay soil, as they have a tendency to rot easily.

The best thing is to dig out a trench or a hole where you want to put your bulbs, and put the soil in a wheelbarrow or tub. These plants like to be planted from four to six inches deep, so dig out to a depth of at least eight inches.

Start refilling the planting hole with a couple of inches of sand or perlite for good drainage, then half fill with some compost and stir this mix together. Finally, top up the hole with enough of the originally-removed soil to fill it. Add a handful of organic slow-release fertilizer for each plant you're putting in the hole, and then stir up the layers a bit with a garden fork or trowel.

Then you can make individual planting holes in this new soil for each of the bulbs or plants. If you're planting new bulbs, they should all be about three to four inches deep. For the plants you started indoors, put them deep enough so their stems are buried a bit lower than they were in their containers. At this time you can also spread the recommended amount of mycorrhizal fungus on the soil. Once everything is planted, water the area really well and mulch the exposed soil.

How do you dig up and store summer bulbs?
Since these summer bulbs can't tolerate the winter cold, they have to be lifted out of the garden if you want to store them for use again next year.

Many gardeners wait until the first frost has touched the leaves of these tender plants before lifting them, but you don't have to wait that long. Once the weather has turned cooler and the plant has gone past its best performance, you can consider taking it out of the ground and getting it ready for the winter.

Use a garden fork to loosen the soil all around the roots of the plants you want to lift. As you loosen the soil, it will become quite easy to pull the plant right out of the ground completely. It's best to work on one colour of one variety at a time, so that you don't get them all mixed up.

Once you've lifted all the plants that are the same type, shake off the excess soil from the roots and cut the stem off the bulb part. You can chop up the stem and foliage into your compost, but put the bulbs on sheets of newspaper to dry overnight. Make sure you identify the separate varieties and colours with labels or tags.

When the tubers have dried, you'll notice that each type of plant has a different shape of root system. But they all consist of thin feeder roots and much fatter bulbs which are the storage roots, and these are the parts we want to keep over the winter.

The storage root of the canna lily is a series of hard tubers, like hairy ginger roots. Once they're dry, you can trim off the small feeder roots and save the fat sections.

The calla lily grows from a hard round corm. When it's dry, you can trim off all the thin feeder roots.

Dahlias grow from tubers that are oval or slightly pointed. Their size depends on the variety of the plant, but can be as small as a golf ball or as large as a small sweet potato. You may find several of them connected at the same point. These can be divided, as long as you cut them so that each tuber has a small section of stem growing out of it.[fig. 31]

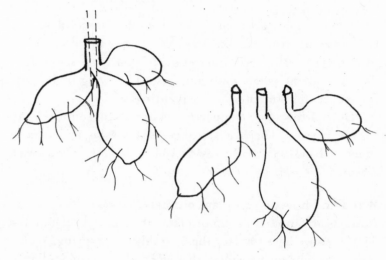

[FIG. 31] DIVIDING DAHLIA TUBERS

Tuberous begonias have golf ball-sized tubers, with lots of feeder roots on the bottom that can be trimmed off when they're dry.

And finally, the gladiolus corm is a bit unusual. The one you planted in the spring will have almost disappeared, while a brand new corm will have grown on top to replace it. Discard the shell of the old one, and save the new one for next year.

Once you've separated all the storage roots, and collected them by colour and type, they should all be dusted with a powdered copper or sulphur based fungicide to protect them during the winter. Coat them well, particularly places where you cut the stems.

Then they need to be stored for the winter. The two conditions that are essential for safe storage are "cool" and "dry." The temperature should be around 8-12 degrees C (45-55F), and the conditions as dry as possible.

One of the best ways to store the bulbs is in paper bags. You can write the variety and colour on the outside, and then put the corms and tubers inside with lots of dry peat or vermiculite around them. This will help to keep them dry all winter.

You can place a bunch of the bags into a larger plastic or cardboard box for safe-keeping. All you need to do is find a place that's suitably cool, and free of rodents. If the tubers look dry next spring when you want to start growing them, soak them overnight in water before planting.

Don't throw away an opportunity to save your summer bulbs for future years. They'll get stronger each season, and some of them will multiply and provide you with more plants each season.

When and how do you plant annuals?
Annuals are another group of plants that cannot tolerate the winter, so we have to plant them freshly every spring. With a few exceptions such as violas, they will do best if you wait until the ground has warmed up before planting them. Most annuals will stay in bloom for the majority of the growing season with very little attention.

Seeds of annuals can be sown directly into the garden in the late spring, but they take time to germinate and grow to a size that's ready to flower. These days we tend to buy ready-to-plant seedlings of annuals that have been produced by specialized growers in the horticultural industry. This may be a bit more expensive than growing from seeds, but it saves a lot of work and gets the garden looking nice as soon as possible.

When you buy ready-to-plant annuals they've been grown with up to a dozen in a box or a cell pack. Those in cell packs are much easier to transplant because each plant can be popped out of its individual division, whereas those in boxes have to be cut apart.[fig. 32]

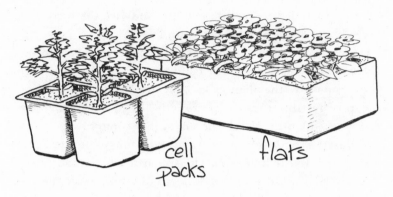

[FIG. 32] ANNUALS IN CELLPACKS AND FLATS

Before planting any annuals in your garden, you should evaluate your soil. If you've followed the techniques described in Chapter One and your soil is a good loam, then skip this next part. If your soil is questionable, you should prepare the planting area first.

Dig out the place where you want to plant the annuals, put the soil in a wheelbarrow or tub, and refill the hole with half compost and half removed soil. The excess removed soil can be recycled through your compost pile.

Spread some slow-release granules of organic fertilizer, as described in Chapter Three. About one small handful for every annual you are planting. Use a rake or fork to stir the fertilizer into the soil surface.

If the annuals are in a cell pack, pop each one out and lay it down. If they are in boxes, use a sharp knife to cleanly cut the roots into squares. (This does much less damage than trying to pull them apart.) Arrange the individual annuals in whatever pattern you want to plant them, because it's much easier to move them around *before* you plant them.

Allow enough space between each plant for it to spread over the season. If you're not sure how wide they will get, refer to the plant tag or look it up in a plant encyclopedia. The natural tendency is to plant them too close together, to try and fill the empty spaces right away. Be patient, and give them room to spread both above and below ground.

Once you've settled on the planting pattern, start planting. Use a trowel, a stick or your hand to make a hole in the soil about the size of the plant's root ball. Into this hole pour about a cup of fertilized water (preferably 10-52-10), which will reduce the planting shock and encourage root growth.

Dust the roots with some mycorrhizal fungus powder, drop the plant into the hole, firm the soil around it, and move to the next plant. Once you've done all of them, water the area gently but thoroughly and cover the exposed soil with mulch.

When and how do you plant perennials?
Perennials are plants that can live through our cold winters. The above-ground portion of the plant dies off, but the roots become dormant and are able to live through the winter. The roots and root crown act as storage organs to provide nutrients to the plant so it can grow new foliage very early in the spring.

Perennials can be grown from seed, but it often takes one or two seasons of growth to produce a plant that will flower. The most common way of producing new perennial plants is through some form of vegetative reproduction, either cuttings from or divisions of larger plants. The horticulture industry has growers who specialize in perennial production, and a very wide variety of potted plants is available through garden centres and markets.

Perennials are usually sold mature enough to flower the same season they are planted, since this is what the gardening public wants. Less expensive plants are a year old, more expensive larger ones are two or three years old. The larger ones will perform better and produce more foliage and flowers right away

When buying new perennials, if you want to get a good clump established quickly, then buy either one large plant or several smaller ones. An odd number of small plants such as three or five is recommended.

Planting perennials is usually done in the early spring, as soon as the ground has drained enough to be dry and workable. The weather is cool and this reduces one of the stresses of planting time. It also gives them a whole season to get established in their new home before the winter rolls around.

Another suitable time to plant perennials is in the early fall, when again the temperatures are cool and the stress reduced. However, there is less time for the plants to settle in before winter.

[FIG. 33] PERENNIAL PLANTING HOLE

When planting perennials, which are going to stay in the same location for many years, the soil preparation is obviously very important. You want to encourage an extensive and wide-spread root growth to support lots of foliage growth, so improving the surrounding area is important.

Position the perennial in its pot where you want to plant it. If you are planting several smaller pots, allow several inches around each plant for them to spread. Then put the pots aside and dig out an area that's about three times as wide as the space they occupied, and about half again as deep. Remove the soil to a barrow or tub.

You should now have a saucer-shaped planting hole. [fig. 33] Fill this hole with a mixture of half compost and half the removed soil, and a handful of organic slow-release fertilizer for each plant. Throw the ingredients into the hole and stir them up.

Now you can dig individual planting holes for each plant, turn the plant out of its pot, and place it in the soil.

If you notice the roots have grown in a circle around the inside of the pot, use a sharp knife to slice downwards through the outer roots every couple of inches around the root ball. This will encourage new roots to grow outwards. [fig. 34]

Position the plant so that it's about the same depth it was

[FIG. 34] SLICING CIRCLED ROOT BALL

in the pot, neither too much higher nor too much lower. At this time you can also spread the recommended amount of mycorrhizal fungus on the exposed roots. Then firm the soil around the root ball so there are no air pockets, water the whole area gently but thoroughly and spread mulch over the exposed soil.

When and how do you plant ground covers?
This group of rather specific perennials is dealt with in Chapter Six, along with that other major perennial ground cover, the lawn.

What are biennials, and how do you plant them?
Biennials are a form of short-lived perennial. They are hardy enough for their roots to live through a winter, but they spend

their first year producing leaves, and only flower in their second year. Then they die.

This process can be confusing because biennials often produce a lot of seeds that start growing during the latter part of the second season, and even though the parent plant dies, more plants grow the next year. Gardeners may be fooled into thinking that the plant is still alive, when it's actually its offspring they're seeing.

Some common biennials are *althea* (Hollyhock), *campanula medium* (Canterbury Bells), *dianthus barbatus* (Sweet William), *digitalis purpurea* (Foxglove), *hesperis* (Sweet Rocket), *and lunaria* (Honesty).

When the small seedlings are seen in the late summer garden, they can be left alone or dug and moved to new locations to perpetuate the plant elsewhere.

As for buying biennials, they are often misleadingly sold as perennials. They really should not be sold at the same price as perennials since they are likely to only live a year.

The planting process for biennials is exactly the same as described for perennials.

When and how do you plant shrubs?

The hardy deciduous shrubs are like perennials in some ways. They can live through harsh winters and they store food in their root systems. The main difference with perennials is that the above-ground stems of shrubs don't die in the winter. Their soft leaves drop off but the tissues of the stems gradually harden each autumn and become able to withstand the severe cold.

Like most trees, shrubs get bigger by increasing the length and girth of their stems each season, rather than spreading and multiplying underground. There are exceptions of course, but aren't there always?

Shrubs are usually acquired by the gardener through purchasing them at a young age from a garden centre or specialized grower. They can of course be grown from seed, but very few of us have the patience to wait the many years this takes. Most shrubs are grown from cuttings taken from growing tips, which are rooted, planted and grown for several years until they reach saleable size.

The smaller specimens of shrubs are usually marketed in containers, which are easy to handle and ship. Larger specimens may be sold with a large root ball wrapped in sacking and rope. This method is known as "ball and burlap" or simply "B & B".

Either way, the purchased specimen should be placed in the ground as soon as is practical in the early spring, while it is still slightly dormant and before the leaf buds have broken open. Fall planting is also suitable, after the leaves have fallen off, but this reduces the time for the plant to become comfortable in its new location and it may be exposed to some stress. Planting during the summer, when the plant is active and with a full set of foliage, is not recommended.

In the same manner as for perennials, the planting hole for a shrub should be a saucer shape. [fig. 35] It should be slightly deeper than the container the plant is in, and several times as wide. Ideally the hole should slope upwards until it's wider than the spread of the stems and foliage of the shrub. This will give the plant plenty of space to grow new roots, which will help to anchor the plant as well as feed it and keep it healthy.

Put the removed soil from the hole into a barrow or container, and then use a garden fork to loosen the soil at the bottom of the hole to make root penetration easier.

Refill the hole with a mixture of half compost and half removed soil. Keep it loose and don't flatten it down too much. Mix in some slow-release organic fertilizer granules, about one cup for every foot of height of the shrub's stems. Stir this mixture together.

Then make a hole in the centre of this area for the shrub, which can be left in the container while you handle it. Make the hole just as deep as the container, so that the shrub will not be planted any deeper or higher than it was before, and a little bit wider.

Turn the shrub out of the container, and if the roots are circling the root ball, use a knife to slice downwards through the outer roots every couple of inches all the way around.

At this time you can spread the recommended amount of mycorrhizal fungus over the whole root ball. Then lower the plant into the hole and carefully fill in with soil all around it. Press the soil close to the plant firmly into place.

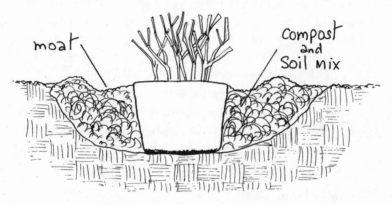

[FIG. 35] SHRUB IN PLANTING HOLE

Now you need to make a shallow moat around the plant. Use some of the leftover soil you removed from the hole, and make a low wall around the plant about a foot away from the centre. Water it gently but thoroughly and spread a thick layer of mulch over the whole area. Concentrate most of the water into the moat you've made.

When and how do you plant vegetables?
Most of the vegetables we grow are annuals, and we'll deal with them first. There are a couple of perennial vegetables, which are dealt with at the end of this section.

Vegetables need to be planted where they will get fully exposed to the sky and sun. Even being in the semi-shade will severely affect their growth. However, during the hottest parts of the summer the leaf crops would appreciate some mild shade during the middle and latter part of the day, either behind taller plants or from a screen of cloth or lattice. These crops soon become bitter and go to seed in the heat.

As explained in Chapter Four on watering, vegetables react strongly to the water supply in the soil. Too little water all the time and your crops will be considerably reduced. An erratic water supply will cause the growth to slow down and then speed up. This causes tomato fruits and cabbage heads to split. What you should be aiming for is a consistent soil water content at all times. Using a mulch really helps to keep the moisture level of the soil in a stable condition. A soaker hose irrigation system takes a lot of the effort out of this situation.

Larger plants are heavy feeders. They will benefit from getting some extra feeding in the middle of the summer and again in the late summer, about a month apart. You can use a liquid organic fertilizer in water, or pull back the mulch and spread some compost over the root area.

Vegetables from seed.
Some vegetables are best grown from seed. The root crops of radishes, carrots and parsnips, the leaf crops like spinach and chard as well as the legumes such as beans and peas are all easily grown from seed.

Peas and spinach don't mind being sown in the cool of the early spring, but all the rest will do best if sown once the ground has warmed up to about 16 degrees C (60 F).

The soil for a seed bed must be worked on to get it into what's called a "fine tilth", which will surround the seeds with a blanket of small particles. The best way to make it is to take a medium sieve and process topsoil through it until you've got a two inch layer of sifted soil on top of the garden. This is your seeding bed.

Use a stick or the tip of a trowel to make a furrow in the seed bed, as deep as is recommended for the particular seed variety on the seed packet. Usually, the larger the seeds, the deeper the furrow. Make the furrow as long as you want the crop to be, and make as many furrows for that crop as are needed. Then drop seeds into the length of each furrow, spaced the distance apart that is recommended on the seed packet. It will usually say something like, "Space the seeds two inches apart, in rows one foot apart."

Cover the seeds with some of the soil, and use a very gentle spray head to water the whole area gently but thoroughly without disturbing the soil.

These instructions refer to a time when vegetable gardens were large and were tended by machines. The rows had to be wide to allow traffic for cultivating. I would like to recommend you try something different, called "wide row" gardening.[fig. 36]

Divide your vegetable garden up into rows four feet wide, with a two foot wide path between each one. You fill each of the wide rows with closely-spaced furrows and plantings, and work on them from the pathways either side. You never walk on the actual beds. As a result they stay un-compacted and you get very high yields. I can't take credit for inventing this method, as it's been around for ages, but I'll keep suggesting it because it works so well.

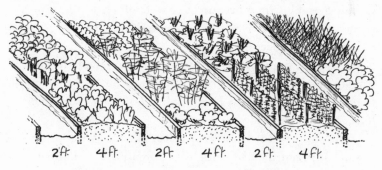

[FIG. 36] WIDE-ROW VEGETABLE GARDEN

When your seeds emerge from the soil, they will probably be a bit too thickly planted for their own comfort. They have to spread roots and foliage, and the mature plant is so much bigger than those tiny things sprouting from the soil.

Start thinning them out as soon as possible, because crowding will only cause reduced growth right away. I know it's hard to pinch off such new life, but you have to be a bit ruthless occasionally.

After a week, when the rows are well established, spread some mulch over the exposed soil between them. Keep the soil well watered, because at this stage the seedlings are very shallow-rooted and any surface drying will harm their fragile root system. But make sure you water deeply each time, so that the new roots are attracted downwards to the moisture, nutrients and safety of the depths.

You can also plant further crops of vegetables from seed during the season. Second crops of bush beans should be started a couple of weeks after the first crop. You can even use the space where peas were growing for this later crop. Some plants, like the leaf crops and peas and radishes, don't do as well in the very hot temperatures of the mid summer, so it's better to start a late summer crop from seed towards the end of the summer.

Vegetables from seedlings.
Other vegetables are more fun to grow from seedlings. It means you're planting a fairly mature plant and you don't have to wait as long for it to become a crop.

The most popular to do this with are larger plants such as tomato, pepper, eggplant, cabbage, broccoli and the squash family. But you can also buy seedlings of leafy crops such as lettuce and romaine.

The soil bed for these crops should be as good as for any annual or perennial bed, with lots of organic matter and plenty of organic nutrients from compost or fertilizer. These plants have deep root systems, so the beds should be dug and enriched to a depth of at least ten inches.

You can also practice the wide row technique with large crops, by staggering the planting pattern and using strong supports to keep the taller ones straight.

Planting seedlings uses the same technique as described for annuals previously. Make a hole, water it, sprinkle mycorrhizal fungus on the roots, and stick in the plant.

Make sure you allow sufficient space all around the plant for it to grow in size. With vegetables you're aiming for the largest, earliest or most prolific results, so don't spoil getting maximum results by crowding your plants.

There's a trick to planting tomatoes that I find very effective. Quite often when we grow or buy tomato seedlings they are a foot or more tall when we come to plant them. You can just stick them in the ground and have really tall plants, or you can take advantage of the fact that tomatoes are able to develop roots all the way along their stem.

If you have a tall seedling, strip off all its lower leaves, only leaving two or three at the very top. Instead of digging a small planting hole, dig a four-inch deep trench about as long as the plant is tall. Lay the plant down on its side in the trench, water it, and cover with soil. Just leave the plant's top three inches (with the leaves) exposed above ground.[fig. 37]

The tomato will develop a lot of roots all along its buried stem, adding greatly to its ability to gather moisture and nutrients. I'm not guaranteeing that you'll have giant plants, but I've noticed that they grow very strong stems and seem to resist drought better.

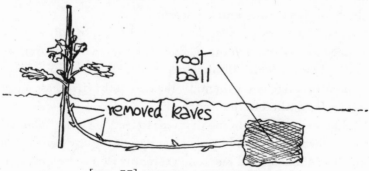

[FIG. 37] BURYING A TOMATO PLANT

105

Leeks are also rather different in the way they are planted. The small seedlings should be planted in the bottom of a six-inch deep trench. Just poke a hole with a pencil and place each seedling in it. As the leeks get progressively fatter, you can fill in a couple of inches of soil at a time into the trench. This will cover the lower part of the leaves, cutting off the light and giving the distinctive white base.

The rest of the allium family are planted from what are called "sets", small versions of the final onion-like plant. All the yellow and purple onions, shallots and garlic are planted this way, although garlic should be planted in the fall and not the spring. The green bunching onions, or "scallions", are planted from small seedlings, rather like leeks. The more you hill soil up around their bases as they grow, the more white flesh you'll get.

Perennial vegetables.
The two main perennial vegetables we grow are asparagus and rhubarb. Once planted in the right place, they can go on producing for years.

Both plants require deep well-fertilized organic soil, so you'll need to dig deep beds with plenty of compost and organic matter mixed in.

Asparagus roots need to be planted in the spring in trenches 18 inches deep, each root a foot and a half from its neighbour in the row. You'll need several plants per person to provide plenty of tips throughout the season.

Place each root crown on a slight mound of soil with its feeder roots spread around it. Put a few inches of soil over the roots and water well. As the stems appear above the soil, fill in with more soil to cover them. By the end of the first season you should have filled in the trench. [fig. 38]

Let the foliage grow the first year to feed the newly-planted root crown. You should only start harvesting the tips in the spring of their second year, and then only for the first month.

Let the following tips produce foliage to keep strengthening the root crown. In the third year, you can cut tips all season long. A well-planted asparagus bed can keep producing for 10 to 20 years. Use a long-bladed knife or special curved asparagus knife to harvest tips below the surface.

When any of the foliage starts to produce seed pods, cut it down because the scattered seeds will become a nuisance.

If you want white asparagus, it's not a different variety. Just hill up soil around the tips as soon as they start emerging, keep them covered, and the lack of light will keep them white.

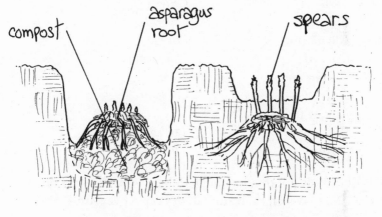

[FIG. 38] PLANTING ASPARAGUS ROOTS

Rhubarb roots should be planted in the spring in wide holes about six inches deep, spaced about two feet apart. Place the root section in the hole with its feeder roots spread out around it so the top of the crown is just beneath the surface. If there are bright pink buds growing from the top of the root crown when you get it, these should be allowed to poke up out of the soil.

Each spring spread generous amounts of compost around each plant if you want them to keep producing thick stems. When harvesting, pull rather than cut each stem.

Individual rhubarb plants should be lifted and divided every three years to keep them from getting crowded. Do it in the fall, and cut each large root crown into several pieces, but each one has to have a couple of pink buds visible.

When and how do you plant herbs?
Herbs are either annual or perennial. Both should be planted in exactly the same way as described for annual and perennial flowers in this chapter.

Here's a list of popular herbs, showing which are annual and which are perennial in our Canadian climate.

Annual herbs	Perennial herbs
Basil	Chives
Borage	Lavender
Chamomile	Lovage
Chervil	Marjoram
Coriander	Mint
Dill	Oregano
Parsley (a biennial)	Sage
Rosemary	Tarragon
Savoury	Thyme

Rosemary is not tough enough to be a perennial in a sub-zero climate, so treat it as an annual, or keep it over winter indoors.

When and how do you plant seeds?
In our Canadian climate, seeds can either be planted directly into the ground in the spring, or they can be started indoors ahead of time.

Some plants, notably a few vegetable varieties, germinate quickly and grow quickly to maturity from seeds and can be planted outdoors and harvested during the growing season.

However, many other annual and perennial flower seeds are much slower to get started and take quite a while to become mature enough to flower, so if they are planted outdoors this slowness defeats their purpose. In which case they can be started much earlier indoors, and can be planted outdoors in the spring as seedlings.

Growing from seeds outdoors.

Earlier in this chapter was a description of starting vegetable seeds outdoors, and similar methods can be used if the gardener wishes to grow flowers from seed.

Growing from seed indoors.

Many Canadian gardeners chose to grow plants from seeds indoors. Some for the fun of it, many to save money on buying seedlings and others because they can't find the exact varieties or colours of seedlings they want at garden centres or markets.

Vegetable varieties such as tomato, pepper, cabbage, squash and leaf crops such as lettuce are very easy to germinate and grow this way. The same applies to most of the annual varieties of flowers that we like to have.

Perennials are a different story. Some of them require certain specific triggers, such as time or periods of exposure to cold temperature, in order to break their dormancy and get them to germinate. Others are as easy as annuals. It all depends on the variety. If you plan to grow a particular perennial from seed, I would advise finding out as much as possible about its special germinating requirements. It will save you a lot of heartbreak.

For example, varieties such as *delphinium, dictamnus, gentiana, hemerocallis, lavandula, penstemon, phlox, primula, rudbeckia* and *viola* all need to be treated to several weeks of near-freezing temperatures after they've been planted in damp soil. To artificially simulate the passage of a winter buried under a layer of snow, gardeners have to plant the seeds and put them in a refrigerator for four to eight weeks before they are ready to germinate.

However, once you're ready to raise some plants from seeds indoors, it's not that difficult. I would encourage every gardener to try it, at least once, with something easy. Tomatoes are a favourite, because it's hard to find seedlings of all the great varieties that are available from seed.

There are a few key requirements. You need some space that's not disturbed, that can be kept in the cool 18 to 21C range (65-70F) and that can provide plenty of strong light. This latter is essential for small seedlings, as the proper light level will make them grow strong and compact and start them off with a big advantage. If you have a set of four-foot fluorescent lights (with two or four tubes) there's no limit to what you can grow. If you've only got a sunny windowsill, then your options are a bit more limited but still viable.

Also remember that two dozen seeds planted in a tiny container will grow up to be 24 seedlings, each in its own pot and all of them occupying considerably more space than you may have imagined. I would recommend that you lay out as many three-inch pots as you can provide good light for, and limit your actual seed planting to the same number.

As for when to start each type of seed, here are a few general guidelines for someone who will need the seedlings to be ready to plant in the garden at the beginning of June.

Perennials, start in January and February.

Annuals, start in February.

Large vegetables, start in March.

Small leaf vegetables, start in April.

If you want to approach seed growing with a high degree of success, I'd advise getting set up properly right from the start. I'll explain my own system of growing plants from seed, and you can either follow it or make your own adaptations.

I use 11 by 22-inch trays to hold all of my seedlings. They're a standard size and containers fit in them nicely. For the actual seeding I use cell-packs with six divisions. This limits the damage during transplanting. And for the final growth of the seedlings I use three inch pots. Nearly two dozen of them fit into each tray.[fig. 39]

For a mixture to plant the seeds into I've opted for one that's completely soiless. This removes a big problem for the very small germinating seeds, as they are very susceptible to

110

dying from a "damping-off" fungus found in soil. My home-made seeding mix is composed of four parts milled sphagnum moss, two parts vermiculite and one part perlite. This gives a spongy mix that holds moisture well, and is very easy for tiny roots to grow into.

I fill each division of a cell pack with the seeding mix, press it gently down until it fills about three-quarters of the depth. Then I place my seeds on the surface of the mix. If I have lots of seeds I place three or four. If the seeds are expensive and I have only a few, I place only one per division.

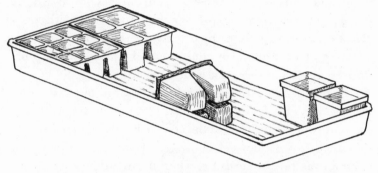

[FIG. 39] PLANTING TRAY, CELL PACKS, THREE-INCH POTS

Then I cover the seeds with as much mix as is needed to have it at its appropriate planting depth. Each seed packet will provide the "planting depth" for that variety, but as a rule of thumb it's about three times the diameter of the seed. Large seeds are therefore planted deeper than small ones. And very small seed that's hard to see can be sprinkled on the surface and not covered at all.

I carefully identify what's planted in each division as I do it. This is very important, because it's very easy to get different cultivars of the same variety confused when they're small seedlings. A permanent marker pen on a wooden coffee stir-stick works well for me.

The cell pack is then dunked into a tray of water to let the seeding mix soak up as much moisture as possible. Moisture is the real trigger that gets seeds sprouting, so this step is critical. It's also important not to let the cell packs dry out during the time that the seeds are germinating. I cover them with a sheet of dry-cleaner bag plastic, or with the clear plastic covers from bakery products and salad mixes. (Reuse, recycle!)

Next comes the germinating period. With fresh seeds it can be as little as a few days for some annuals, up to a couple of weeks for some perennials. The most ideal situation is to have the seeds exposed to warmth from underneath, referred to as "bottom heat". The heat, up to 25C (80F), speeds the germination, and coming from the bottom encourages downward root growth right away. You can provide this bottom heat with special electrical heating pads, or by placing the tray of seedlings over a source of heat or warm equipment. I use the flat top of a fluorescent fixture which is gently warming.

Be patient with this part of the operation, but at the same time be vigilant. As soon as you see any sprouting activity in even one of the divisions of the cell pack, take it away from the germinating area and get it into the light. This is the most critical time for the seedling, when it can either start life as a compact tough little plant, or as a long lanky and rather weak one.

You'll notice that the first set of leaves that poke up may not look anything like the real leaves of the plant you're growing. They are the cotyledons, who's job it is to push up to the light. They will be followed by the first of the "true" leaves.

Let the seedling grow for two weeks, or until it has developed two true leaves, and then transplant it out of the soiless mix into some real soil and into a larger pot. The plant is still very young, but I've found that there's much less risk of damage to the fragile root system moving it now than later. This is where I use the three-inch pots, and I fill them with a potting mix that's three parts potting soil, two parts vermiculite and one part perlite.[fig. 40]

I use a tool like a tongue depressor to ease the seedling out of the cell pack with all its seeding mix attached, and drop the whole plug into a three-inch pot half full of potting mix. I then fill in carefully around the seedling with more mix, dunk it in the water tray, and put it back into the light.

That's it. The plant then has to be watched, watered whenever it gets too dry, and kept as cool as possible. Warm temperatures will make it grow soft, so cool conditions under 21C (70 F) with a slight breeze from a fan will toughen it up nicely.

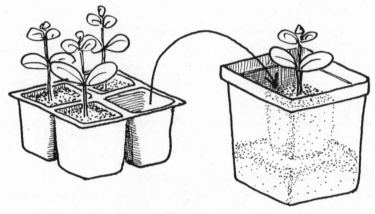

[FIG. 40] FROM CELL PACK TO POT

In your own method you can replace cell packs with small pots, you can replace sphagnum moss with peat moss or a pre-mixed packaged seeding mix and you can replace anything else you like with your own version. It's the basic principles that count. Things like cleanliness, soilless mixes, proper temperatures and vigilance.

Hardening off seedlings.
The next major step you should worry about is getting the plants "hardened off" before you go and stick them in the ground in the spring. Growing indoors has not exposed the seedlings to the wind, rain and blustery conditions of our outdoors in the spring. So they need a period to become gradually accustomed

to the outside world. Unhardened plants will get a shock that will set back their growth and perhaps even spoil them for the whole season.

If you can spread the hardening off period over a couple of weeks it would be ideal, but it can be compressed into a week if absolutely necessary. Start by taking the plants outside for an hour or so, into a shaded place that's protected from wind and rain. Gradually increase the length of time of this daily exposure, and also increase the exposure to the sun. Do it as gradually as possible.

After a week when they're staying out all day, you can consider leaving them out all night, but only if the temperatures stay above 10C (50F). If not, bring them indoors for the night. By the end of two weeks your plants should be ready for transplanting into the garden, under normal weather conditions. They will still need some protection from extreme cold, hail and deluges of biblical proportions.

When should perennials be divided?
As far as the actual time of the year to do this work, it's best in the early spring, before a lot of stem and leaf growth has started. It also avoids any serious impact on their growth and gives the divided transplants a chance to get established before the heat of the summer.

You can also divide some varieties in the late summer and early fall, particularly those that bloom very early in the spring. This avoids disrupting their blooming period, and you're doing the work when flowering and new growth activity is over. They should be given plenty of time to settle in before the winter.

The one time to avoid dividing and transplanting is in the middle of their growing period, and at times of hot weather when they face a lot of stress from high temperatures.

As for when a particular plant needs to be divided, perennials grow in size at different rates so you'll have to judge accordingly. A clump of peonies, for example, takes several years to increase appreciably in size , and seldom needs to be split up to reduce its spread. On the other extreme, hostas spread remarkably quickly, and within a couple of years could be spreading beyond their bounds.

There are other varieties, such as phlox and iris, which spread outwards from their original planting leaving behind an unproductive centre to the clump. Every few years they need to be dug up and the newer sections replanted to maintain the vigour of the clump.

The best indication a plant needs dividing is when its growth starts to have an impact on its neighbouring plants. If a clump starts to overshadow surrounding plants with its foliage, or moves into the space and crowds out another, then it may be time to take action.

If your intention was to let a particular variety spread to take over a section, then you should move the others out of its way. If, however, you set up a planting plan by carefully positioning various plants and taking into account their bloom times and heights and colours, you may not want one particular variety to become too large or too dominant.

∾ LIST OF PERENNIALS THAT SPREAD QUICKLY ∾
Achillea, alchemilla mollis, anthemis tinctoria, aubretia, arabis, euphorbia polychroma, ferns, helenium, hemerocallis, hosta, iris, liatris, ligularia, monarda, oenothera, phlox, physostegia, saponaria, sedum, stachys lanata, verbena, veronica. Several herbs such as marjoram, oregano and thyme are spreaders, and of course all of the ground covers described in Chapter Six.

You may also wish to divide a perennial for no other reason than to multiply it, and to get other clumps of it spread and established around the garden. It's a good idea to wait until a plant is two or three years old and producing lots of new root growth before you start hacking it up, but it's a very valid reason for dividing.

How to divide and transplant perennials.

Fortunately, the vast majority of perennials can be divided in a very similar manner. It involves dividing their root crowns to produce small sections that can be started as new plants. The object is to break or cut apart the crown so that each section contains several buds (where the stems and leaves come from) and a good supply of the roots needed to nurture the plant.[fig. 41]

You may need any of the following tools at some point, so it's best to be prepared: a small pocket knife, a long-bladed kitchen knife, a small pruning saw, pruning shears, heavy gloves, a garden fork and some sort of strong tarpaulin as a work surface so you don't make a mess everywhere.

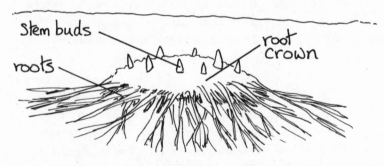

[FIG. 41] PERENNIAL ROOTCROWN, ROOTS, BUDS

It's always best to dig up the whole plant when you plan to divide it, even if you want to keep some in the same location. It means you can work on the plant with less damage, and it also allows you to replenish the soil before replanting the "mother" plant. If you're dealing with a very large clump, this removal can be a two-person job.

It's also good to do this sort of work on a cloudy day, as there's less risk of drying out any exposed roots and also less stress on the transplants.

Use the garden fork to gently loosen the soil all around the root ball, and for at least a foot outwards from the plant. This reduces the damage to the roots when you lift the plant.

Lift the whole clump onto the work surface, and decide how much of it you're going to remove. A large clump can be initially loosened by pushing two forks back-to-back down though the crown so you can gently lever apart a couple of smaller sections, but do it slowly and try not to tear too many roots.[fig. 42]

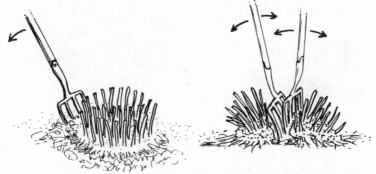

[FIG. 42] DIGGING A CLUMP AND DIVIDING WITH FORKS

You'll find that most root crowns are made up of many individual pieces, each with buds on the top and roots coming out of the bottom. If you can use your hands to gently pry apart smaller sections of the crown, it's much better than cutting and causing wounds. However, some parts may be joined at the top and need to be cut with a knife, shears or saw.

As you pull apart sections, lay them aside for replanting. If this operation is taking some time, cover them with wet cloth to stop them drying out.

You may notice that older parts of the crown are not producing buds. Lift out the clump, break it apart, remove the dead sections and replant. Always look for buds, which are usually most active on the outer edges of any crown.[fig. 43]

Once you've got the divisions you need, you can replant the mother plant and transplant the new sections. Each planting hole should be prepared as described earlier in this chapter under "When and how do you plant perennials?"

When it comes to planting the pieces you removed from

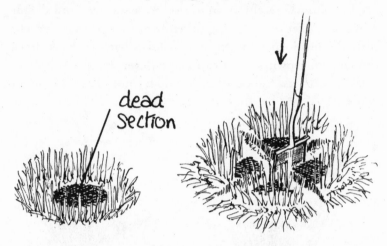

[FIG. 43] BREAKING APART DEAD SECTIONS

the mother plant, to start new clumps growing, make sure you plant enough to have at least three to five buds on the new crown. You can plant a lot more if you wish, but you should start with at least this many to ensure a plant of substantial size.

As you settle each section in place, make very sure that the roots are spread out and the buds are just at the surface level.

Two exceptions to this rule. The peony requires the buds to be planted two inches below the surface. The bearded iris likes to have its tuber half in and half out of the soil.

Make sure you put soil around the roots without leaving any air pockets, and once the hole is filled in you can press firmly downwards to settle the soil. Water the area gently but thoroughly, and if you see the soil has subsided a bit, add some more to nearly cover the buds. Mulch the root area.

There are many variations of this basic dividing technique that you'll have to learn to tailor to suit different varieties of perennials. They are just too numerous to mention individually. But the theory of dividing small sections with buds or miniature plantlets from the parent plant still applies. The division will always need a section of crown with some buds and some roots.

six

Lawn Care

Lawns have become so much a part of our gardens that it's hard to think of a home without one. Even if a homeowner cares little for the fine points of the more decorative arts of gardening, there's probably a well-kept lawn surrounding the home.

There are some who feel lawns consume far too much fertilizer and energy being kept in perfect condition. But in defense of the lawn, the millions of small grass plants produce huge amounts of oxygen for our urban environments, and along with trees are absorbers of large quantities of pollution.

There are ways we can practice more environmentally sound lawn maintenance techniques, and that's what I'll concentrate upon in this chapter.

What makes a good lawn?
As with anything else in the garden, good soil is the key to a good lawn. An ideal lawn soil would be a clay loam that's at least ten inches deep, with broken up sub soil beneath it.[fig. 44] This will allow good moisture retention, good drainage and a depth that will attract deep root growth.

Deep roots are the key to survival for a lawn, particularly when there's a prolonged dry spell. During a drought you'll see some sections of your lawn turning brown before the rest, and those are the areas with the shallowest root systems. The grass goes dormant and turns brown, but its growth will revive as soon as moisture returns.

We often inherit a lawn from the previous owners of the

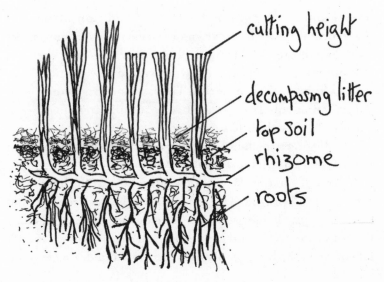

[FIG. 44] GRASS PLANT GROWTH

[FIG. 45] BUILDING A GOOD LAWN

home, and know nothing about the condition of the soil underneath. Older lawns are more likely to have a substantial layer of good top soil that's built up over time, but they can also suffer from compaction. Lawns around newly-built homes may have been laid on a thin layer of soil over compacted construction rubble and clay. Lawns in hilly areas may be on rocky ground with little surface soil.

So digging a small hole with a spade is a good idea to get an idea of what's down there. Make a one foot square hole about a foot deep, if you can. Have a look at the sides of the hole to see the actual soil profile. The top layer will be dark topsoil, and next will come lighter soil, etc. The deeper the topsoil layer, the better the lawn. And the deeper you can dig before you hit lots of rock, the better moisture retention and drainage you'll have.

You should also be able see how deeply the grass roots have penetrated. Three to four inches from the actual surface is not bad, but anything deeper is much better.

What can I do about poor lawn soil?
The simple answer is to gradually improve the soil over the years. You can do this every spring by applying an inch of compost, or a mixture of half-and-half peat moss and topsoil. This will gradually build up a better layer of soil for the roots, which will gradually grow deeper over time.

If your lawn is one of the unfortunate ones with a very shallow layer of soil over poor conditions underneath, your options are less simple. You can work on it gradually, as described above, and be prepared to water a lot during dry periods. Or you can truck in six or more inches of new soil and start all over again.

When and how do you plant a new lawn?
The best time to build a new lawn is in the very early spring. Grass plants grow fastest when the conditions provide cool

nights and warm days, with plenty of moisture, which is in the spring and fall. But to give the plants a full season of growth it's best to do the seeding early in the spring.

Lawns need a well-prepared soil bed to get started. You've got to take into consideration the fact that these are perennial plants that will be in their home for many years to come. So the preparation should quite thorough. There are many ways of doing this, but I'll describe a method that most people can manage without breaking either their back or their bank account.

You should wait to work on a lawn area until the garden has dried out enough so that traffic won't compact the earth and ruin it.

The existing ground of the area should be turned over with a mechanical cultivator, to break up the surface and disturb the sub soil as much as possible. Try to level the broken soil over the area as much as possible, as this will avoid high and low spots later.

Then spread a layer of compost or shredded organic matter three to four inches deep. Next comes a layer of topsoil at least four inches deep, but more if you can afford it. These layers will settle lower, so having more really helps. Spread granular slow-release organic high-nitrogen lawn fertilizer in the amount recommended by the manufacturer on top of the soil. (Don't use a chemical fertilizer in the first year as it may be too harsh for the young plants.)

Then go over the surface with a garden rake, removing any twigs and stones, scratching in the fertilizer and smoothing the whole area level.[fig. 45]

At this point you should roll the lawn to settle the soil into place. Owning a lawn roller has gone out of fashion, but you can rent one from garden centres or tool rental companies. For this job, fill it about one third full of water so it provides just enough pressure evenly all over the lawn. (For a small area being seeded, you can use a board, the back of a rake or your feet to firm the soil).

Now you have the option of either spreading grass seed or laying sod. Grass seed is much less expensive for a large area, but requires work to spread and takes time to mature. Sections of sod make an instant lawn, but large quantities require professional delivery and laying so they are expensive.

Seed

If you plan to use grass seed, buy the best (see "What's the best grass seed to use?")). It should be spread evenly over the area, and using a mechanical seed dispenser makes this job a lot easier. Garden centres will often lend you one when you buy a lot of grass seed. To make sure it's evenly distributed, split the amount of seed in half and spread the first half up and down the lawn, and the second half from right to left across the lawn.[fig. 46] And save a little of the seed for repair jobs, so that you can match the same sort of mixture as the rest of your lawn.

At this point you really should roll the lawn to settle the soil and the seed into place.

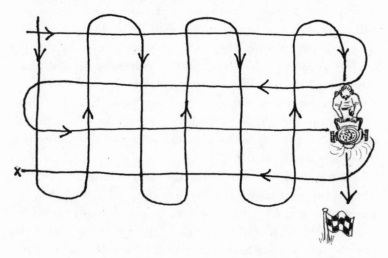

[46] LAWN SEED SPREADING PATTERN

Now all you have to do is make sure your seed is watered every day to get it germinating and producing deep roots. If nature doesn't provide rainwater on schedule, you'll have to do it by hand, not with a sprinkler. Use a spray nozzle on a fine mist setting. This will not disturb the seeds in the soil, unlike the typical lawn sprinkler. Don't let the soil surface dry out for at least a month, as the germinating seeds are at a fragile stage.

You'll soon see a green haze cover the new lawn area, as the seeds sprout and send up their first small blades. Keep up the watering every few days if it doesn't rain, until you see full-sized leaves and plenty of them.

The first mowing of your new lawn should wait until the grass is about four inches high. It's very important that you use a mower with very sharp blades at this point, because blunt ones can pull the young plants right out of the ground in patches.

Sod

As mentioned above, laying sod is a professional job. There are companies that specialize in this, growing their own sod grass to meet their own standards. There are also companies that mow farm fields and "strip mine" the top few inches of growth and call it sod. If you want to avoid the latter, deal with a garden centre or landscaper you trust or one with a reputation to uphold.

The sod comes in six foot lengths, rolled up, and should be laid the same day it's delivered. Each roll should be full of moisture to keep it alive, so each one is quite heavy and a lot of them are usually piled on pallets on the truck. It's a job for equipment and people with strong backs.

If you have a small repair job, needing just a few rolls, you could do it yourself. If so, lay the sod on a well prepared bed (as above), and lay them in a brick pattern, so that the seams overlap.[fig. 47]

After laying, all the seams around each section of sod should

125

be filled with topsoil to stop the edges from drying and dying. Sod laid on a slope should be held in place with wooden pegs until the roots take hold.

Water the new sod as it's being laid, and then again twice a week for the first couple of weeks, until you see that it's growing (a good sign that it has rooted well.) Don't mow until it has grown four inches high.

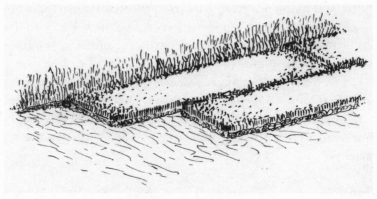

[47] SOD-LAYING PATTERN

What's the best grass seed to use?

When buying grass seed you should be looking for three things; the quality, the variety and the type.

Quality

For an assurance of good quality, grass seed sold in Canada should be labeled "Canada Number One." What this means is that the product has been inspected to see it contains a very high percentage of seed and not chaff, that it's the variety it claims to be and that it contains little or no weed seeds. Look for this on the label.

Variety

There are three principal varieties of grass suitable for lawn use in our climate, not to be confused with the tall ornamental types. They are fescue, Kentucky and perennial rye. Within each variety are many named cultivars with different growth properties.

Grass seed packaged and sold here usually contains a blend of at least two of these varieties, preferably three, with one cultivar chosen from each group. The percentages of each are clearly marked. This not only gives a rich looking lawn as a result of some variety, but it also protects against the lawn being wiped out if one variety is attacked by disease.

When shopping, look for blends that contain a fescue, a Kentucky and a perennial rye. If you see the name "annual rye grass", that's alright as long as it's a fourth part of the blend. As its name implies, annual rye only lasts a year and then dies. It's often put into a mix to provide a grass that's "first up" in the new lawn, providing some leaf cover and roots to hold against erosion while the slower varieties follow. But don't go for a grass that has more than 25 percent annual rye.

Type

You may see a confusing selection of packaged grass seed mixes when you go shopping. They will likely have all sorts of enticing descriptive names to tempt you to buy them.

However, all you should be looking for are two criteria. Are they designed for full sun or semi-shade areas, and are they for high or low traffic areas?

Grass will not grow in full shade, no matter what the package tells you or the name implies. It just won't work. There are some cultivars suitable for semi-shade, and that's the best you can hope for. If you're struggling to grow grass in the shade, stop struggling and go to the section in this chapter on "ground covers".

So if it says it's good for "shady" conditions, it means semi-shade. Just about all the rest are for full sun.

That's when you can look for a mix that's best for the traffic your lawn will bear. The manufacturer selects different cultivars within each variety and tailors each mix for different purposes.

Do you have young children, teenage soccer teams, large dogs or frequent garden parties on your lawn? That's a high-traffic area, and there are some tougher grasses more suitable for this. You can also ensure a stronger lawn by spreading the grass seed as heavily as you can afford.

If, however, you only occasionally play a spirited game of croquet or wander around admiring your delphiniums sipping a glass of Pimm's Number One from your lawn, then a lesser-traffic mix is fine for you.

What is "over-seeding"?

If your lawn is looking a bit thin, from poor fertilization or being cut too short, you can strengthen the mat of roots and the leaf coverage by adding some more plants to the lawn. This is done by over-seeding.

As the name implies, you're adding seeds over the existing lawn. This is done by spreading the appropriate seed type at about half the usual rate. You can do it over large sections, or over specific areas where traffic may have weakened the growth. However, for serious problems with high-traffic areas you should also see the section dealing with compaction in this chapter called "Why won't my lawn grow well?"

For over-seeding to be effective you should spread the seed, immediately followed by a top dressing with sieved compost or a peat and top soil mix to cover the new seeds. Water every couple of days for a month to encourage the new seeds to germinate and take hold.

How do you repair bald spots?

I've been asking my barber that question for years. But on the lawn it can be done with a mini version of the same routine used to lay a new lawn.

First of all, loosen up the underlying soil with a garden fork to aerate it. Spread a two inch layer of topsoil, then a good sprinkling of grass seed. If you have some of the original seed you used on your lawn, that's great. If not, buy a small bag of a suitable blend. Press the seed firmly into the topsoil, then keep the area watered for the next three or four weeks.

This same routine should be applied when you clear out a bunch of weeds and leave a bare patch. Get grass seed established as quickly as possible, so that new weed seeds don't take root.

What should I check for on the lawn after the winter?

As the lawn wakes up from the winter freeze, you may see some damage right under the snow as it melts. Look for round grey or pinkish patches of what's called snow mold. This is a fungus which thrives in the almost-zero conditions under the snow as it melts into very cold water, and sits on the still-frozen lawn surface.

It can show up where snow was packed down (due to footprints) or piled up deeper (where it was thrown) and therefore takes longer to melt.

There is no magic spray treatment for this fungus. Use a lawn rake to gently disturb it when the sun is shining, as this helps to stop it growing.

What can I do about thatch?

Another problem might appear in the early spring is thatch. This is a layer of dead grass, which is what will remain if you didn't keep cutting the lawn quite short in the fall, right up until the ground froze hard. The longer blades will have died during the winter, packed under the snow, and now form a rather compact mat of pale dead grass blades.

Thatch is unsightly, and it interferes with new grass growth. It reduces the flow of air and water to the roots, and it can harbour insects and disease.

The solution is to remove it, but not by pulling it up. That might pull up living roots along with it. The correct way is to slice it into short lengths with a de-thatching tool.[fig. 48] This looks a bit like a rake, but it has a series of sharp blades instead of tines. As you drag it across the lawn it slices the dead grass lying flat, but doesn't harm the roots or new vertical blades of grass.

For very large areas you can rent a de-thatching machine, with spinning disk blades that do the same thing.

Once the thatch has been cut, it must be collected with a rake and disposed of on the compost pile.

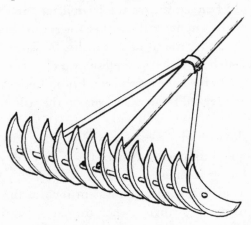

[FIG. 48] DE-THATCHING RAKE

What can I do about compaction?

Another early spring situation to watch for is soil compaction. When lawn soil becomes compacted it really interferes with grass root growth, and this affects the quality of the lawn. It also slows water and air penetration with similar results.

Compaction isn't that obvious to the eye, but there are signs you can look for. If people create a pathway across a part of the lawn with constant foot traffic and wear out a track in the grass, the soil gets compacted. If perennial weeds like dandelion and plantain grow a lot in one place or along the edge of a path or driveway, it's because they can out-compete grass in compacted soil.

In both of these places if you use a thin probe to test the density of the soil, you'll probably that find it's harder than

130

the rest of the lawn.

To combat compaction you need to aerate the soil for several inches. Aeration for a small area can be done with the tines of a garden fork. Plunge the fork into the soil, and pull it back and forth to create small holes. Do this closely-spaced all over the area, then spread some topsoil or compost to fill the holes loosely. For a large area, you can rent a mechanical aerator. It's like a roller with spikes and rolls over the lawn digging out narrow plugs of sod and dropping them on the lawn. Rake the plugs to break them up and get the loose soil spread into the holes.[fig. 49]

[FIG. 49] FORK AND MACHINE AERATION

If your compaction was caused by feet, consider paving what people obviously already consider a path. If you have a weed problem, dig them up, aerate and reseed.

When should I feed the lawn?

Lawns should be fertilized early in the spring, so that the active grass growth has access to plenty of nutrients.

If you regularly spread compost over your lawn every spring, and leave the clippings to decompose naturally, then your lawn probably doesn't need any fertilizing at all.

If you don't do that, then you should spread an organic

fertilizer to give it a boost as soon in the spring as the lawn soil has drained and dried out enough to safely be walked upon.

You can use a granular slow-release type, spread by hand or with a mechanical spreader. (Garden centres will often lend you one when you buy the fertilizer.) Calculate the quantity recommended for a lawn of your size, and spread half of it up and down and half of it right to left.

You can also apply the fertilizer as a liquid. Some concentrates are sold in a container with a hose attachment. You screw it onto the end of a water hose and as you spray the lawn, a measured amount of fertilizer concentrate is sucked up and mixed with the water.

The only other time a lawn should be fed is in the fall, if you've just laid sod or seed and you want to encourage root growth. Spread a fertilizer high in phosphor (P) such as bonemeal, rock phosphate or a blend like 2-10-5. Don't waste time spreading much nitrogen, as it will be washed away during the winter.

How much water does a lawn need?

On a weekly basis a lawn needs an inch of water, either from rainfall or from your irrigation (see Chapter Four).

In the spring this is most often provided by the weather, but not always. It's a good idea to keep track of the rainfall each week either through weather service data or by measuring it yourself. As has been mentioned in Chapter Four, you can buy a rainfall gauge or you can use a coffee or tuna tin to measure the depth of rain. [fig. 50]

During the hot summer period, some municipalities impose water-use restrictions and these are aimed particularly at lawn watering. You should stick to your allotted watering time, which you can do even if you're away by using a timer. Make sure you measure the application over a particular time to see that you apply at least your inch per week.

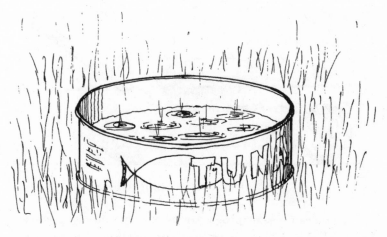

[FIG. 50] MEASURING LAWN WATER

What's the proper way to cut a lawn?

If you're using a lawn-cutting service, it's much more difficult to control just how your lawn is cut. You don't always have a say in how the job is done. Some home owners have been able to get co-operation by explaining the reasons behind their specific requests, but others haven't. All you can do is try.

Your objective is to keep the grass a bit longer than you would find on the greens of a golf course. You're aiming more for what it's like on the fairway. The ideal is to cut a lawn down to two inches, let it grow for a week, and then cut it down to two inches again. This two inch height is very important for several reasons. [fig. 51]

By keeping the lawn that long, you're letting the grass blades be stronger than any small weed growth. The length is also shading out newly-germinated weed seeds and stifling their growth. During the hot sunny weather you're also shading the grass roots and reducing water loss from soil evaporation.

When you get to the dry times of mid summer, you can certainly see the difference between a lawn that's been scalped short and one which has been left longer. The very short grass dries and turns brown so much sooner.

[FIG. 51] MEASURING BLADE HEIGHT

As you can see, keeping your lawn longer doesn't mean any less work. You still have to have cut it as often, but you just don't shave it like a putting green. If you explain to your lawn-care personnel that by asking for them to cut it longer you're not telling them to cut it less often, perhaps it will sound less threatening.

The main resistance to getting co-operation seems to be false perceptions. There's fear that you're asking for less frequent cutting and that a longer lawn won't look as if it has been cut. These misconceptions should be carefully debunked, and you can point out that the lawn-care company can actually benefit. They can explain to their other customers how they're "...instituting a new cutting policy which will result in stronger healthier lawns. All part of the service!"

However, if you're cutting the lawn yourself then you have complete control over how it's done and should aim for perfection.

Start off by using a "reel" mower if you can. The blades spinning against a fixed plate cut the grass tips much more cleanly than the slashing action of the helicopter blades on the rotary mower, which just slash the grass.[fig. 52] If you don't believe me, try this test. Two days after a lawn has been cut with rotary blades, get your eyes down to ground level and look along the very top of the lawn. You'll notice a slight brown haze. What you're seeing is that each grass blade has a small brown tip where it has died back, after being shredded by the rotary blades.

Unfortunately, motor-operated reel mowers for the home-owner are rare or very expensive. You see large ones at golf courses, where they already know the value of this type of mower. But until someone markets an inexpensive motorized version here, we can only buy the hand-operated ones.

If you have a large lawn you'll probably be forced to use an electric, gasoline or ride-on mower, and then you're stuck with the rotary blade types. You can still adjust the height of the cut up to two inches on all these machines, and you should do so immediately. If the machine doesn't have the actual cutting heights marked on its adjustment system, you can measure it yourself. Measure from the bottom of the wheels to the lowest edge of the blades, and adjust until it's two inches or just over.

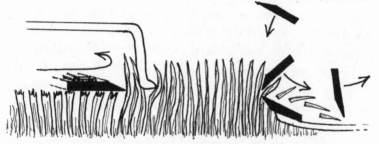

[FIG. 52] ROTARY AND REEL MOWERS CUTTING ACTION

How can I keep the edges of my lawn cut properly?

Because of the way the wheels of a mower are positioned, they always keep the blades from cutting right to the edge of a lawn. This means that you have to follow each cutting with a second operation on the edges, using hand-operated lawn shears or a wire trimmer.

It also requires the occasional use of an edging iron or spade to trim the edges cleanly and keep the roots from invading the adjacent bed. [fig. 53]

This can be avoided if you install what are referred to as

"mowing strips". These are sections of brick, stone or paver, a minimum of 7.5cm (3 inches) wide. They are laid along the very edge of the lawn where it meets garden beds or other obstacles, to make a solid non-grass edging.[fig. 54] It allows the wheels of the mower to stay level along the very edge, and gives a space where there's no grass to cut. These strips should be laid into the soil in the same manner as any other hardscaping, with landscape cloth first to block roots, then some grit and sand to seat the stones.

What should I do with the grass clippings?
Grass clippings can normally be left on the lawn to decompose naturally, adding their nutrients back into the soil. But this only works well if the clippings are short, when you're mowing your lawn regularly.

If the clippings are over a couple of inches in length, they should be raked up and put onto the compost. Bits longer than that left on the lawn will form a dense mat, and they won't decompose easily. You'll end up with a sticky mess, or thatch.

There are some mechanical mowers which have a feature whereby the grass clippings are held in the cutting chamber for a moment or two longer than normal. This allows them to be shredded even more, so even quite long clippings are chopped into very small pieces. This feature is usually referred to as a "mulching" action, and is quite useful to have.

Why won't my grass grow well?
There could be many reasons for poor grass growth, so the answers will be equally varied. Perhaps it's as simple as the fact that you've never fertilized it. (See earlier in this chapter.)

Shade
The most common reason for poor grass growth is shade. This is usually caused by trees overgrowing the lawn area, causing deep shade for most of the day. If the trees are very close to the

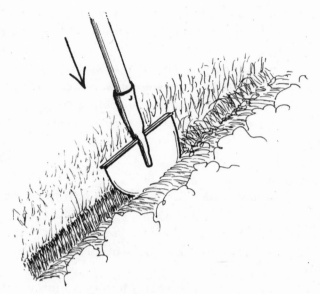

[FIG. 53] TRIMMING EDGES

[FIG. 54] DIFFERENT MOWING STRIPS

lawn, the grass roots may also be in serious competition with the tree roots for moisture and nutrients. It's a battle the grass will always lose.

This is something you can't fight by adding more soil or more grass seed. You have two solutions. Either cut down the tree (not always a good idea) or you could grow plants more suitable than grass in that area. (See "ground covers" later in this chapter.)

Compaction

Another common cause for poor grass growth is serious compaction of the soil. It will stifle grass growth completely. You should first understand what caused it in the first place (foot traffic, vehicles, play, etc) so the problem can be avoided in future.

Serious compaction will need a lot of aeration to loosen the soil to a depth of a foot or more, and then grass seed and topsoil could be spread. This work was described in more detail earlier in this chapter under "What can I do about compaction?"

Poor soil

This is a catch-all reason, covering all sorts of ills. But the main reason is that the soil itself is generally not hospitable to plant growth.

If it's not caused by shade or compaction, but grass and other plants refuse to grow, then you may have some toxic soil. This could have been caused without your knowledge at any time. For instance, perhaps workmen spilled waste that turned out to be toxic or altered the pH so drastically that it's deadly to plants.

Or perhaps something underground has percolated upwards. I have a patch in my garden which was where the Victorian owners of the house dumped their coal-fired furnace ashes. Everything planted over it suffered badly, until deep digging found the problem. Now it's a brick-covered area for container plants.

Your options for solving a poor soil problem can range from digging out the offending dirt and replacing it, to building something over it so plants that are never put in it.

How do I get rid of the weeds in the lawn?

Lawn-care companies can promise you weed-free lawns because they spray with products called "selective herbicides." These particular poisons kill all the broad-leaved weeds in your lawn (and elsewhere), but don't kill the narrow-leaved grasses.

However, many municipalities are restricting and regulating the use of these herbicides on lawns, because of concerns over health issues. Even one whole province, Quebec, has severely restricted the type of herbicides allowed to be used by anyone other than farms and golf courses.

So for anyone facing these restrictions, or who never wished to use these selective herbicides in the first place, the choices of how to get rid of weeds have always been fewer and harder.

A problem with a few dandelions can be handled with one of the many weeders that are suitable for this deep-rooted perennial. [fig. 55] All it takes is a bit of time spent looking for

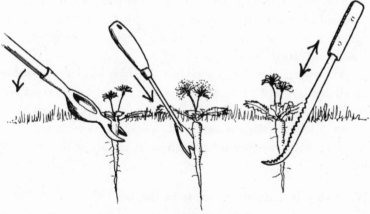

[FIG. 55] WEEDING TOOLS

them and removing them. Plantain is rather like the dandelion, but not as deep-rooted so they come up much more easily. Always seed a bare spot left after weed removal, so that you establish grass in its place.

Things get a bit more difficult when your lawn has a lot of a weed such as "Creeping Charlie," or *glechoma hederacea* as it is formally known. This round-leaved plant has very shallow roots which spring from each leaf node as it comes in contact with the ground. As its name implies, it can creep into everything. Eradication is hard, even with chemicals. It can be pulled up easily, and must be attacked as soon as it is seen. You can keep it in check somewhat by not mowing the grass too short.

But a lawn that's badly infested with Creeping Charlie or any other weeds may need drastic measures to remove them. Your only alternative may be to kill off everything and start fresh.

There are some herbicidal products that will kill plants, which are still allowed under even the strictest regulations. That's because in themselves they're not that harmful to the environment. Some organic herbicides contain acetic acid and are made from lemon juice and vinegar. Others use various fatty acids from soaps. These are NOT selective and will kill off everything, weeds AND grass. So if you use them on an infested area, rake off the dead plants, prepare the ground and spread seed or sod (as described earlier in this chapter) and start with a fresh lawn.

I know that weeding a lawn is hard work, but let me say that a well-fed lawn with grass that's never cut too short is very much more able to withstand the usual incursions of weed seeds. And if you quickly repair any situations where stress can encourage weed growth, you should be able to maintain a very natural weed-free lawn.

What should I do about moss in the lawn?
Having patches of moss growing in your lawn is a sign of two things. There's either too much shade in that spot, or the lawn

is less fertile than it should be and the grass was overcome by the moss.

The solution to the former problem is to either remove the shade or don't try to grow grass in that spot. For the latter problem of fertility, just scrape off the moss, roughen the soil with a rake, spread some granular organic fertilizer and then some grass seed.

Why do mushrooms grow in my lawn?
First of all, the conditions have to be right for mushrooms to grow. They like warm moist soil, so this can happen any time during the summer.

But the fungus will only grow if spores have taken root. This usually happens if a mushroom cap grew in the same location and was allowed to deposit its spores last year. Or you may find that a fungus spore host, such as a piece of rotten tree branch, is buried just beneath the soil surface.

Either way, the best defense is to cut off the head of the mushroom as soon as it emerges from the soil, to make sure it doesn't cast its spores around. This may not solve the long-term problem, as more may emerge later, but you can stop it from getting worse.

Why do I have to clear dead leaves off the lawn?
It can be a never-ending job to keep clearing the dead leaves off the lawn in the autumn, particularly when some kind soul next door uses a leaf-blower to send their leaves over to your property.

But it's a job which has to be done. Dry leaves don't decompose very quickly just lying on a lawn, so they tend to stay where they fall for a long time. If there are many of them, forming a dense mat, they cut off the air and water circulation to the soil below with disastrous results.

If you leave them on the lawn until the snow covers them, the same situation happens with even worse results. The snow can't melt away as it should into the lawn, resulting in flooded patches and more possible dead grass.

So get the leaves cleared off the lawn as soon as possible after they've fallen. If you line the leaves up in long rows, you can use your lawn mower to shred them. Then they can be used in your compost or buried in the soil of the garden to rot away and add all their organic matter.

If you have too many for this, donate them to your local municipal composting program by filling the appropriate bags for pick-up.

What are "ground covers"?

There's a group of particular perennials that are usually referred to as ground covers. As their name implies, they spread low to the ground and form mat-like growth.

The most famous perennial ground cover is the grass we use for lawns, but grass isn't always a suitable plant for some locations. Perhaps there's too much shade for grass to grow or too steep a slope for it to be conveniently mowed or you'd like to get rid of some lawn and replace it with other perennials.

Fortunately, most of the plants we categorize as ground covers grow well in full or semi shade, which is why they're so useful instead of grass. Many are shallow-rooted too, which means they can usually compete quite well for food and water against the heavy root systems found under the trees that often are the problems creating the shade.

Here are some of the more useful perennial ground covers that tolerate shade: *ajuga reptans, convallaria* (lily-of-the-valley), *lamium, pachysandra and vinca minor* (periwinkle).

For sunnier conditions you can try these low-growers: *alyssum saxitale, aubrieta, iberis sempervirens, cerastium tomentosum, dianthus, hedera helix, lysimachia nummularia, phlox subulata, saxifraga, trifolium repens* (clover), herbs such as marjoram, oregano and thyme.

One plant that is often listed as a ground cover is *aego-*

podium podagraria, known as Bishop's gout weed or variegated ground elder. NEVER use this invasive weed as a ground cover, unless you are prepared to see it spread everywhere into flower beds and lawns. It spreads via shallow but persistent roots, which are almost impossible to dig up without leaving a few behind to keep growing.

If you ever need to plant something that must be kept within boundaries because of its invasive habit, such as mint or gout weed, surround it with a deep edging material to keep the roots inside. But be vigilant, because these plants have an uncanny ability to worm their way out of barriers.

[FIG. 56] GROUND COVER PLANTING PATTERNS

When and how do you plant ground covers?

Planting perennial ground covers is done in the same way as planting any other perennial, as described in Chapter Five. The best time is in the spring when the soil has warmed.

Since you normally want quite a few individual plants to cover an area, ground covers are usually sold in trays of 24 or more "plugs". These are narrow seedlings ready for planting, and they should be spaced about six inches from their neighbours in an offset planting pattern.[fig. 56]

By their nature, ground covers are shallow rooted, so you should make sure they get plenty of water for the first few months in their new home.

To make sure that they will spread quickly and not face competition from weeds, you should mulch the area after planting the plugs.

SEVEN

Controlling Pests

Pest control is a sensitive subject. When we start to try and control things like insects, which account for over two-thirds of all animals on the earth, we're messing with nature in a big way.

Even dealing with it as a subject for gardeners, on a very small scale, we run into a lot of questions. When is an insect a pest? What is its function in the greater scheme of things? Why are we so keen to get rid of it? How are we going to do it? What am I doing that might effect the environment in a negative way?

All of these questions have ethical implications, some of which are beyond the scope of this book. But for the average gardener, all we want to do is have a nice-looking bunch of flowers and harvest a reasonable amount of the crops we plant. And I'm going to assume that we'd all like to do it with the least amount of negative impact on the environment in which we live.

So all of the pest controls mentioned in this chapter are what I believe to be the best available in the "environmentally sensible" category of controls. Hopefully, more will arrive on the market as soon as possible. Researchers, and more importantly manufacturers, realize that the gardening public is much more interested in low-impact controls these days, and is willing to put up with more work in return for less destruction.

On top of that, many municipal and provincial governments have instituted regulations on the use of pesticides which are quite restrictive. They only allow pesticides from an approved list to be used, and only if a serious infestation can be proved.

This has forced the horticultural trade to provide more "organic" pest controls, and it has actually spurred the growth of a whole new part of the industry.

However, this still doesn't answer the basic question of what impact we as gardeners are having on the environment when we use a pest control. My answer to that is as follows.

If you're fighting a losing battle with a pest, and have used all of the non-invasive techniques and home remedies, then perhaps it's time to use a product designed to help you. But when it comes to choosing that product, you should select it from the list of "organic" controls that will have the least impact on the environment while doing the job. In that way you're hopefully part of the solution rather than part of the problem.

What are pesticides?

"Pesticide" is a very general term for anything that helps to control a pest. It may seem obvious to some people that you don't use an insecticide to control a fungus, but it's not obvious to all. So here's a brief explanation.

Within the general group of pesticides are subdivisions which describe the nature of the control.

Insecticides control insects.

Fungicides control fungus.

Herbicides control plant growth.

Acharicides control spiders, ticks and mites.

Rodenticides control mice, rats and other rodents.

Molluscicides control slugs and snails.

Vermicides control worms.

Products within these groups may prevent, control or destroy a pest, depending on the pest and how the product works. Using a product from one group will usually not help to control a pest in another group.

How can you tell if you have pests?

A healthy garden has very few pests. Strong plants can resist or withstand some attacks, and a healthy garden has a mixture of fauna that prey upon each other to maintain a natural balance.

It's when plants become weak that they are likely to become unhealthy. They become more susceptible to a disease taking hold or an insect becoming an infestation.

So the first line of defense is to keep your plants well fed, well watered, well groomed to encourage good air circulation and to keep the whole garden clean of debris.

However, in spite of our best efforts, there may come a time when you realize that something is wrong, and some action is needed. The best response is to act fast while it's a small problem and to be thorough in your treatment.

Here are some of the things I recommend as a way of being aware of what's going on in your garden.

Check frequently. You should tour your garden often, with your eyes wide open and your glasses on if necessary. Don't stop to do all the jobs you see need doing, because you'll never make a complete round if you do. Just go around first, looking for any small discrepancies in growth, any marks that shouldn't be there, any disturbances of the soil or foliage which indicate that something has been around. Don't be an absentee landlord.

Identify the problem. Since pest controls only work if they are directed at the right pest, you have to be sure of what you are seeing. Don't just react if you see a bug. There are thousands of them in your garden, most of whom are there to help you. It's when you see damage or a pest that you know, that you should start reacting. Identify the damage correctly (spots, trails, blotches or holes) and try to link this damage to a particular pest. If you can find this pest nearby, there's your suspect. But don't forget that many insects are nocturnal, so you may not see them during the day.

Accept some damage. This may sound foolish, but before you reach for a poison or get involved in a lengthy treatment procedure perhaps you should accept a modest amount of damage. If an insect is making some holes in a decorative plant towards the end of a season, unless you're number one in the local garden tour coming up maybe you can leave it alone. But if you see the start of a problem that you know is going to spread, such as evidence of fungus disease or aphids, then by all means react.

Use the right control. Once you've identified the problem, you may have several options for its control. Start with the least invasive and see if it works before you move on to others. This will be your way of working *with* the environment rather than against it. Make sure you pick the correct action or product to counter the problem. Don't spray with something just because you own it. There's not one product that's a magic bullet for all problems. Make sure you follow the correct procedure for that particular control, whether it's the strength and frequency of an application or the temperature or timing considerations. Otherwise you could be wasting your money and not controlling the problem.

Treat what's necessary. Because one iris is showing signs of leaf miner, it would be prudent to check all your other clumps of irises for the same problem. If you're treating for fungus on one lilac shrub, perhaps all your others should be given a preventative fungicide spray too. However, having said that I'm not advocating widespread use of a control unnecessarily, particularly when it comes to some of the stronger organic pesticides. You can treat only an affected plant if you don't see the problem elsewhere.

Keep the garden clean. Many problem pests find homes in your garden in places that you provide. Slugs stay nice and damp during hot days, hidden under foliage debris or boxes left to one side. Squirrels are attracted by fallen fruit left on the ground. You may be inadvertently allowing them to hide from their natural predators. Or you may be spreading a disease by not clearing up infected foliage.

Offer other temptations. If you want to see how many slugs there are in you garden, put out a saucer of stale beer one night. In the morning you'll see just how many were visiting that area of the garden. Don't be afraid to leave nearby wild areas populated with what you might consider weeds, since they'll attract both the predators and their prey. Putting sugar water traps for wasps and yellow sticky traps for aphids and whitefly is fair game too, as this will not only remove them but will give you an idea of how many there are around. Planting more crops than you need is another way of making sure you get what you want, even if you have to share them.

What's the difference between organic and chemical pesticides?

I'd like to put in a word about terminology here. We tend to use the words "organic" and "chemical" to distinguish between the two opposite approaches to pesticide sources and manufacturing. I intend to continue using these two terms for the sake of simplicity.

What's suggested in these terms is the implication that one is better than the other for the environment. This implication may or may not be correct. I'd like to think that we're approaching pest control in a more sensible manner than in the past, but we've been proven wrong before and may be again.

Using the term "organic" when related to pesticides has become a metaphor for "harmless to humans" in many peoples' minds. However, it should be pointed out that they're not all harmless. Anything that eventually kills an organism is potentially harmful, and should be treated with respect. I draw your attention to the fact that *rotenone,* which is derived from botanical sources, has recently been linked to possible causes of Parkinson's disease. Other naturally-occurring pesticides can be harmful if ingested or if they come in contact with the eyes or lungs. So be as careful when using "organic" pesticides as you would with any other type.

Organic pesticides are the polar opposite of chemical ones in several respects. They usually target a very specific pest, unlike the broad-spectrum chemical poisons. They usually only work in contact with the pest and don't linger in the environment, as opposed to chemical ones that can stay around in the food chain for a long time. And they often work because of their physical properties or their specific impact on the pest, rather than their deadliness to all life.

Let me give you some examples. Horticultural oil used as a spray to combat aphids isn't a magic elixir. It simply coats the bodies of insects and eggs to kill them in a purely physical attack. Similarly, diatomaceous earth is composed of minute shards of silica (like glass) which puncture insect bodies and dehydrate them.

However, there are some poisonous organic sprays too. Insecticidal soap affects an amino acid in the stomach of its targets, so they die of hunger. *Bacillus thuringiensis* (Bt) and *bacillus popilliae* are bacteria that kill very specific pests and leave others alone.

In spite of this rather targeted approach to pest control, organics can be harmful to beneficial insects too. Bt can kill butterfly larvae along with the spruce budworm, and rotenone may harm aquatic life. So we still have to be careful when using them not to upset the natural balance of the garden.

What are some organic pesticides and how do they work?
Many organic pesticides come from botanical sources, derived from parts of plants, and were found when gardeners or researchers observed their impact on insects. Others come from mineral, bacterial and viral sources and were deliberately designed or accidentally discovered to affect pests.

Here are some of the more common organic pest controls on the market today. These refer to the generic name or ingredient, as opposed to whatever name the manufacturers have given their versions. Look carefully on the lower section

of a pesticide label, usually in very fine print, for the actual
active ingredient in the product.[fig. 57]

Don't forget that you can often deter or destroy pests with

[FIG. 57] PESTICIDE LABEL

your own home-made concoctions before resorting to manufactured ones. Refer to the section in this chapter on "home-
made pesticides."

⁓ ORGANIC PEST CONTROLS ⁓

Bacillus thuringiensis (Bt) are bacteria which attack the
stomachs of the larval stage of moths and butterflies. It works
on pests such as caterpillar, cutworm, looper, hornworm and
budworm. It is usually sold as a concentrate that must be mixed
with water and sprayed on contact with the insects. They stop
eating and die after a couple of days.

Bacillus popilliae (milky spore disease) are bacteria that
attack the larval stage, or grubs, of Japanese beetles and June
beetles. A powder or granular mix is dusted on the soil or lawn

over the areas affected. It should be applied in the late spring before grubs emerge as adults, and should be repeated annually in our climate.

Boric acid comes from borax, and is a useful poison against cockroaches and a deterrent of ants. Since it is also toxic to mammals, it should be handled carefully.

Copper has both insecticidal and fungicidal properties, but is most often sold for fungus protection. It is sometimes mixed with lime to increase its effectiveness against fungus. It is most useful dusted or sprayed on foliage to prevent the spread of fungus problems such as leaf spot and powdery mildew, used either as a powder or in a water spray. It should be applied on susceptible plants *before* the fungus takes hold. Apply with care and avoid contact or breathing dust. Very toxic to fish.

Diatomaceous earth is made from crushed diatoms, which become sharp shards of silica. These puncture soft insect bodies causing them to dehydrate. May also be mixed with a poison such as rotenone to ensure a faster action. Affected areas must be dusted to contact the insects, and it must be reapplied after rain.

Mineral oil (horticultural oil) makes use of its coating ability to cover and suffocate insects on plants. It is useful against aphid, whitefly and corn worms. A very fine-textured and purified formulation is needed for plant spraying applications.

Neem is named after a tree found in India and the southern United States. Since very little research has been done on this product, the reasons for its effects are not well documented. Its taste deters some insects from attacking plants, and can also affect their life cycle. The chemical has not been licensed as an official pesticide in Canada, so it is usually sold as a "leaf cleaner". It works well against aphid, whitefly, moth, leaf miner, thrips and many beetles. Concentrates made from the seeds of the tree are mixed with water and sprayed on the affected foliage.

Nematodes are microscopic worms, some of which do

damage to plant roots, but others are useful parasites and are sold as a control for beetle grubs in lawns. They enter the larval stage of the insect, release poisons that kill it and then move on to find other hosts. Nematode larvae are sold in the dormant stage, to be mixed with water and sprayed onto the lawn. This should be followed by spraying with water to help them penetrate to the correct depth.

Pyrethrin is a contact poison extracted from pyrethrum daisies. Since it kills a wide variety of insects and may be toxic to mammals, you should handle it with care. Usually sold as a powder for direct application or mixing with water for a spray.

Rotenone (derris powder) comes from the ground root of a plant, and is a wide spectrum poison that works on beetles. It is toxic to mammals, and can harm fish in ponds, so extreme caution should be taken if using this product.

Soap sprays take advantage of the fact that soapy coatings can smother insects. But research has shown that soaps made from certain fatty acids also have insecticidal properties. They attack certain stomach enzymes and cells of sucking insects such as aphid, whitefly, mealybug and thrips. As a result, several insecticidal soap concentrates are available, to be mixed with water for spraying. The tissue of some plants such as beans and ferns are sensitive to the soap, so test the spray on a small area first. As a result of this, some other soaps have been formulated as herbicides.

Sticky traps can do two things: tell you how many insects are around, and also trap them. Yellow sticky paper attracts and traps whitefly and aphids. A particularly sticky product called "Tanglefoot" can be used to stop leaf miners from climbing the trunk of trees.

Sulphur has both insecticidal and fungicidal properties, which is why it is sometimes sold as a combined fungus and insect treatment. It is sometimes mixed with lime to increase its effectiveness against fungus. It is most useful dusted or sprayed on foliage to prevent the spread of fungus problems such as leaf spot and powdery mildew. Used either as a powder or in a water spray. Should be applied on susceptible plants *before* the fungus takes hold. Apply with care and avoid contact or breathing dust.

Weed killers (herbicides) are broad-spectrum, meaning they kill all plants. Strong solutions of salt water or salt crystals are useful on paths, because they poison the soil for many years. Products based on acetic acid (vinegar, lemon juice) or fatty acid-based soaps are effective against perennial lawn weeds, and soon break down safely. But these must still be used with caution around valuable plants.

How do you make home-made pesticides?

There are several home-made versions of pesticide sprays that you can try before resorting to more poisonous ones. Soap is often added to make the spray cling to leaf surfaces. Here are a few recipes.

Baking soda fungicide for precautionary use against black spot and mildew. Mix one tablespoon of baking soda in one litre of water and shake well. Warm water helps it to dissolve faster. Then add one teaspoon of liquid dish soap. Spray all surfaces of problem plants *before* the fungus takes hold.

Garlic spray concentrate can work against aphid, whitefly, cabbage and tomato worms. Put three crushed garlic cloves into enough mineral oil to cover them, and soak over-night. Then in a separate container put one teaspoon of liquid dish soap into half a litre of water. Mix the garlic-soaked mineral oil in with the soapy water, and store in a sealed container. When you want to spray, add two tablespoons of the garlic spray concentrate with half a litre of water and spray all surfaces of the foliage.

General-purpose bug spray can be effective against chewing and sucking insects such as aphid, chafer, whitefly and thrips. Blend one whole garlic, one small onion and a tablespoon of cayenne pepper in a food processor. Add to one litre of water and mix well. Let stand for one hour. Strain the mixture through a fine sieve or cheesecloth. Add one tablespoon of liquid dish soap. Spray all surfaces of affected plants every two days. Store refrigerated for up to a week.

How do you control specific insect pests?

This is by no means a comprehensive list of what can invade your garden and find it a delicious treat. I have only included the pests that we run into most commonly.

Pest controls for insects span a range of options. You should always start with the option that has the least impact on the ecosystem and if necessary, graduate to the ones with more impact. For instance, start by picking or knocking insects off a plant before you spray with an organic insecticide.

The "Controls" are listed as a series of alternatives. They usually start with the least invasive or simple physical controls (e.g. "hand remove" or "spray with water"), and then move on to more aggressive organic chemical controls. If more than one alternative is available, all are mentioned.

Pest: Aphid (many varieties), a.k.a. plant lice.

Hosts: Young tips of plants (flowers, vegetables, and shrubs).

Damage: Adults suck juice from leaves and stems, causing mottled markings, secrete liquid "honeydew" which attracts ants and fungus. Can transmit disease between plants.

Controls: For eggs: Wipe leaf and stem surfaces with a soapy cloth to remove eggs. Spray with horticultural oil in early spring to smother eggs (best used on shrubs).

For adults: Spray with water to dislodge. Use yellow sticky paper to attract and trap. Spray with insecticidal soap or neem. Dust with diatomaceous earth.

Pest: Ant
Host: Not often found on plants.

Damage: Ants are not pests. They seldom cause damage to plants. On occasion they may collect and protect aphids to eat the "honeydew" excreted by the aphids.

Controls: If you control the aphids (see above) the ants will move on. Ants are very useful predators in the garden, and should not be attacked. If ants become a nuisance indoors, they can be discouraged with borax in crystal or spray format.

Pest: Beetle (various types).
Hosts: Mostly prey on other insects, a few plants.
Damage: Seldom do serious damage to plants, but might discolour some leaves. Mainly feed on eggs and larvae of other insects.
Controls: Not often needed. Flea Beetles can be controlled with diatomaceous earth, rotenone or neem. Japanese Beetles and June Beetles are best controlled when they do damage underground in their larval stage (grubs) with milky spore disease (*bacillus popilliae*) or nematode treatment. Must be applied in late spring/early summer while grubs are active.

Pest: Borer (larval stage of several insects).
Hosts: Trees, vegetable crops.
Damage: Bore into and enter plant stems, causing wilting.
Controls: Watch for evidence of wilting. Look for the entrance hole in the stem near the ground, slit open the stem just above the hole and kill the borer. Cover the wounded stem with soil.

Pest: Caterpillar, looper, hornworm, budworm (larval stage of butterflies and moths).
Hosts: Trees, shrubs, vegetables.
Damage: Eat whole sections of foliage, fruit.
Controls: Physical removal of nests (dispose of by burning or drowning). Spray target foliage with garlic/onion/pepper mix to discourage being eaten. Spray larvae with Bt (*bacillus thuringiensis*) or neem.

Pest: Cutworm (larval stage of moth).

Hosts: Young flower and vegetable seedlings.

Damage: Chew on and cut stems of seedlings just below the surface.

Controls: Place foil or plastic collars around seedlings at planting time, extending two inches underground, to protect the stems. Mix moist bran with Bt and spread on the surface a week before planting.

Pest: Earwig.

Hosts: Decorative and vegetable plants.

Damage: Minor foliage damage from young. Adults scavenge through garden debris.

Controls: Not often needed. Can be deterred with diatomaceous earth.

Pest: Grubs (white with dark head).

Host: Grass roots.

Damage: Chew roots and kills patches of lawn.

Controls: See controls for Japanese and June Beetle.

Pest: Leafhopper, spittlebug.

Hosts: Garden plants.

Damage: Small numbers of insects cause very little damage. Can sometimes transmit disease causing stunting, discoloured leaves.

Controls: Spray with water to remove. Dust with diatomaceous earth for major infestations.

Pest: Leaf miner (larval stage of fly).

Hosts: Some trees and decorative plants.

Damage: Larvae tunnel between tissues of leaves, causing pale tracks.

Controls: Remove affected leaves and destroy. For trees, place a sticky band around the trunk in spring to trap the crawling stage. Spray with neem.

Pest: Lily beetle (like a lady beetle but without spots).

Hosts: Lily stems and leaves.

Damage: Slug-like larvae eat the foliage, adults eat the foliage. Plants can be stripped in a few days.

Controls: All stages must be attacked as soon as possible to stop the breeding cycle.

For eggs: Surrounded with black slime, should be wiped off with a soapy cloth.

For larvae: Remove with water spray. Dust with diatomaceous earth or rotenone.

For adults: Physical removal (destroy or drop into soapy water). Spray with neem. Dust with diatomaceous earth or rotenone.

Pest: Slug.

Hosts: Plant foliage.

Damage: Chew holes in foliage at night, leaving slime trails.

Controls: They prefer smooth damp surfaces, so surrounding plants with dry wood ash or grit can slow their passage. Stale beer in saucers will attract them to drown. Salt burns them if applied directly. Copper mesh or strips will deter them. Granules of iron sulphate and bait (sold commercially) placed in covered traps will attract and kill them, and last through rainfalls.

Pest: Thrips (always referred to in the plural).

Hosts: Flowers and foliage of ornamentals, vegetables.

Damage: Scrape plant skin and suck sap. Nymphs and adults cause streaks and blemishes on flowers, twisting and distortion of leaves.

Controls: Spray with insecticidal soap or neem. Dust with diatomaceous earth or rotenone.

Pest: Whitefly.

Hosts: Flowers and vegetables.

Damage: Adults suck juice from leaves and flowers, causing spotted appearance.

Controls: For eggs: wipe underside of leaves with a soapy cloth to remove.

For adults: Cover any infested plants with large plastic bag to trap adult flies from moving to other plants, and then spray with insecticidal soap or neem.

What about using predatory insects as a control?

Using bugs against bugs is often referred to as Integrated Pest Control (IPC) or Integrated Pest Management (IPM). The theory is if you have a particular insect problem you release a predator that's specifically interested in that insect, and won't do any other damage. It lasts as long as there's a food supply (the problem bug) and then dies off.

There's nothing wrong with having lady beetles released to go after aphids, in theory. For greenhouses where the ecosystem is very controlled, this solution makes a lot of sense and avoids expensive spray controls.

But in a garden environment it doesn't always work so well. The predator insects don't always hang around to find *your* pests, and may soon be off chomping away on your neighbours'. It's an expensive experiment for the home gardener, and of questionable value.

How do you control fungus problems?

The most effective way to avoid fungus infestations is to avoid the conditions which encourage them. It's not possible to control the damp weather, but you can avoid spraying plant foliage with water unnecessarily, and you can avoid crowding your plants which reduces air circulation.

It also helps to catch fungus attacks as soon as they start and never let them go any further. This means quickly cleaning up and destroying diseased foliage as well as using fungus control products.

Growing disease-resistant varieties also helps, as does

spreading mulch to reduce the spread of fungus spores from soil to foliage.

Pest: Downy and powdery mildew, black spot, leaf spot (all forms of fungus disease).

Host: Various ornamentals, vegetables. Most active during periods of wet weather, both cool and warm.

Damage: Gradually harms plant tissue. Leaves fall, fruit and flowers can be affected. Spreads quickly once established.

Controls: For prevention, avoid spraying water on foliage, keep plants un-crowded, and pruned to be open to air circulation. For treatment, use sulphur-based and copper-based spray, or for mild infestations a mix of baking soda in water may suffice.

Pest: Wilt disease (resulting from fungus). Most common varieties are verticillium (V) and fusarium (F).

Host: Tomato family (non-resistant varieties).

Damage: Blockage of water-conducting tissue causes parts of the plant to die. Usually starts with lower leaves which shrivel and die, and gradually works upwards through the whole plant. Fruit may be able to ripen in spite of this.

Controls: No direct controls possible. Remove any affected foliage and destroy. Plant in different locations on a three year cycle. Plant wilt-resistant varieties (shown as "V, F resistant").

How do you control weeds?

The most frequent demand for weed control relates to lawns, where perennial weeds such as dandelion and Creeping Charlie are very common.

Unlike many of the chemical lawn herbicides which only affected broad-leaved plants, organic weed controls are broad-spectrum, meaning they will affect all types of plant life and must therefore be used selectively. You have to spray directly onto the weeds, wait a few days for them to die, and then replace the dead foliage with grass seed or sod (see Chapter Six). Major lawn infestations may require the digging and replacement of large sections with grass.

Organic weed control in the ornamental and vegetable garden should never require the use of herbicides. Start by pulling out any weeds by hand, or cutting off the tips of weed seedlings with a sharp hoe. Avoid the heavy "cultivation" of soil with hoes and other tools as this disturbs the soil structure, loses moisture and exposes buried weed seeds to germination.

The best insurance against weeds in the garden is to use plenty of mulch, starting as soon as the ground has warmed up in the spring. Any perennial weeds which push their way up through the mulch can be spotted easily and pulled out right away.

Pest: Weeds (perennial and annual).
Host: Exposed soil, lawns.
Damage: Compete for valuable moisture and nutrients, spread more seeds.
Controls: Spread a thick layer of mulch on exposed soil in the early spring to smother seedlings and stop new seeds landing. Pull out by hand. In lawns, weeds can be hand dug or pulled. Serious infestations can be sprayed with organic herbicide or smothered, to be replaced with new soil and seed (see Chapter Six).

Pest: Quack grass.
Host: Lawns and meadows.
Damage: Clumps grow faster than surrounding varieties, have less attractive foliage and produce copious seed heads.
Controls: Cut down foliage to expose the root crown and apply an organic herbicide. May require a few applications to kill completely. Carefully dig up the dead clump with its roots, and replace with more desirable varieties.

How do you control animal pests?

We share our environment with the animals that inhabit it, from the deer and groundhogs in rural areas to the raccoons and squirrels that live in our cities. Sometimes they become pests, using our gardens as a food supply. But remember, they're just doing what comes naturally to them.

If it becomes necessary to deter and discourage these visitors, it should be done humanely. However, it will require a lot of cunning because these four-legged pests are intelligent and persistent. There are no magic potions or fool-proof methods for keeping them out of the garden. Often it's a matter of trying several methods one after the other as their effect wears off, or trying a whole bunch at once.

However, after suffering from the ravages of deer in a country garden for years, all I can say is "good luck" and keep trying.

Pest: Deer.

Host: Anything that attracts them. Anything.

Damage: From nibbling of tips to complete destruction.

Controls: A series of different methods done one after the other seems to be the best approach. As they get used to one after a couple of weeks, you switch to another. Here are some of the recommended methods. They run from the least expensive (and least effective) to the most expensive (and most effective). Hang pie plates or CD's to twist in the wind. String fishing line around the protected area, about three feet off the ground. Wrap kerosene-soaked cloth around sticks and place the sticks around the garden. Hang up bars of Irish Spring soap (because they don't like it too!). Hang up bunches of human hair. Spray patches with the urine of dogs, wolves, mountain lions or tigers (I'm not saying this is easy, just that it's been reported to work!). Water sprayers controlled by motion sensors. Deer repellants made with foul-smelling mixtures, to be daubed on plants or on sticks. Fences, either eight feet high (if vertical), or six-strands spread over ten feet and placed at a 45 degree angle. Two parallel four-foot high fences placed six feet apart. Dog patrols between the fences. Live mountain lions and tigers roaming your garden. You get the idea.

Pest: Domestic cats and dogs.
Host: Lawns and tall plants.
Damage: Urine spray which can kill foliage.
Controls: Once the urine spraying starts, the smell will attract them even more. Wash affected plants with a hose. Dilute urine on lawns as soon as possible after it's done. A low fence, even a foot high, is usually enough to deter a passing dog (*and its owner*) from going onto a lawn. There are spray products which use scents to discourage a return to the same place. Water sprayers controlled by motion sensors also work for cats, and they learn quickly not to come back. Lion and tiger patrols.

Pest: Raccoons.
Host: Perfectly ripe fruit (they know the exact moment), insects and grubs in the lawn.
Damage: From small bites to complete loss.
Controls: Not much can deter this curious and nimble predator. Physical barriers such as netting can be set up to protect tomato plants, but protecting rows of corn, berries or grape vines is a major problem. They are not scared of cats, but a dog will keep them away. However, they are most active at night when barking dogs are least appreciated by neighbours. You could try the motion-sensor controlled water spray. Perhaps the foul-smelling deer repellants would keep them away.

Pest: Squirrels.
Host: Some fruit.
Damage: Bitten fruit and flowers, holes dug in gardens

and containers for some purpose known only to the squirrel.

Controls: Physical barriers such as netting over fruit can slow them down. In spring they cut the heads off tulip blooms, and I'm told they are looking to drink the water from the cut stem and not to eat the petals. Put out small bowls of sugar water instead. Dust tulips with a mix of cayenne pepper and chili powder (does not work on squirrels from the Tex-Mex regions!). By the way, I have it on good authority that this mix does *not* cause the squirrels to scratch their eyes out. The water-spraying motion-sensor triggered device will deter them. Dogs and cats also deter squirrels a little, but then I have to re-refer you to "Domestic cats and dogs" above.

EIGHT

Putting the Garden to Bed

At some point in the autumn we have to face the decision to finally stop our gardening activities and prepare for the winter. It's a sad time of the year for a gardener, whether you have a just a few window boxes or a large garden.

Usually it's a touch of frost that puts an end to the growing season, killing off the annuals and burning the perennial foliage beyond redemption for the year. But even if your plants haven't been completely killed by frost, you can still clear them away at the end of the season, and put the garden to bed.

Just a quick word about putting plant material from the garden into the compost. First of all, it should be free of fungus disease, insect pests and any seeds that you don't want to disseminate. And secondly, all the material should be reduced to the smallest possible pieces so it will decompose faster.

Disposing of annuals.
Annual flowers are the first plants in the garden to suffer from the cold weather. Some of them, like impatiens, turn to jelly at the first touch of frost. Others like the marigold are able to withstand a bit more until they too finally succumb to the low temperatures.

We often use the same space where we plant annuals in flower beds to grow spring bulbs, and that's one reason why some gardeners are anxious to remove their bedding annuals as soon as the weather turns cold.

Cleaning them up is quite easy. Just pull them out of the ground, shake off as much earth as possible and throw them on the compost pile. Tear them with your hands or cut them up as you dispose of them.

Preparing containers.

Most container plants are annuals, so they can be dealt with as described above. If you have perennials or shrubs in containers, this will be dealt with at the end of this section.

Once a container has been cleared of its annuals, it should be prepared for storage. Smaller pots and boxes should be emptied of soil (which can go in the compost), and stored where they will be protected for the winter. Clay and other porous containers should not be left outdoors over the winter, as any moisture in the clay will expand as it freezes and cause the material to crumble or crack.

The only containers I'd suggest you don't empty completely are your larger non-porous window boxes and planters. You can certainly empty out the top half of the soil into the compost, but leave the lower half alone. The reason I suggest this is not horticultural, it's financial. Why replace all of the soil mix in a large container, when you really only need to add a few more fresh ingredients to it next spring, and stir it all up into a new mixture.

If you have perennials or shrubs in large planters, they can be left over the winter as if they were in the garden. The perennials should be cut down, and the shrubs given winter protection if needed.

Clearing up the vegetable garden.

Most of the vegetables we grow are annuals, so they die off about the same time in the season as the annual flowers. Plants like tomatoes, peppers, beans and all the leaf crops should be completely harvested, and the roots pulled out of the ground and cleaned of any clinging earth. The non-edible stems and roots should be chopped and put into the compost.

Some vegetables can actually be left in the ground for next

year, such as onions and garlic. There are even some, like carrots and parsnips, which can be covered with a foot of straw and kept in the soil for pulling early next spring. I know some gardeners who even arrange it so they can lift up this covering during the middle of the winter, and pull up helpings of root crops as they need them.

Dealing with herbs.

Herbs have to be handled differently, depending on whether they are annual or perennial.

The useful portions of annual herbs should be harvested and used in small quantities throughout the season. When they are at their peak of production they should be heavily harvested and used or stored. Just before the frost hits them, the remaining foliage should be pulled out of the ground, the useful portions saved and the remainder consigned to the compost.

Perennial herbs should be similarly used as needed, and then harvested in larger quantities when they are at their peak. As the season closes, and just before the first frost, harvest the remaining useable portions of the plants. Any stems or mats of foliage you leave uncut will over-winter under the snow, and re-grow in the early spring.

The one exception to this "perennial" rule is rosemary, which is not quite hardy enough to withstand our freezing winters. You can treat it as an annual and throw it away, or dig up the whole plant and put it into a pot for growing indoors over the winter.

As a reminder, the list of some of the more popular culinary annual and perennial herbs can be found on page 108.

How can I preserve my herbs?

To keep some of your summer supply of herbs for use in cooking during the winter months you can use several different methods, depending on the type of herb and the end use.

To capture the real freshness of herbs, one of the best ways to preserve them is to freeze them. This works for whole sage leaves, springs of rosemary and chopped chives that can be frozen in small portions in freezer bags.

Another way to freeze the more delicate herb foliage is to use the ice cube method. Chop up the herbs and divide them into one tablespoon portions. Put each portion into an ice cube tray section, fill with water and freeze. You can take the frozen "herb cubes" and store them in well-identified freezer bags until needed in a recipe. They may not work as a garnish, but this method is fine for adding to dishes as you cook them. It works well for all herbs.

Finally, the most common way to preserve your herb harvest is to dry and store it in airtight containers. Take branches or sprigs of fresh herbs, tie them in small bundles and put each one in a paper bag with holes punched in it for air circulation. Hang them in a warm place for a couple of weeks until the herbs have dried completely, take out the herbs and crumble the leaves off the stems and store them. Dried herbs are not as strong in essential oils as fresh, but your own dried herbs will be much fresher than the ones sold in most stores. This method doesn't work well on chamomile, chervil, chives, coriander or parsley.

Dealing with perennials.

The majority of perennials should be cut down completely once they've been touched with frost. You can do it earlier than the first frost if you don't like handling dead or soggy foliage. I like to leave a few inches of stem sticking up above the soil so that I can see where they are. This helps to avoid accidents, such as digging into them or treading on them inadvertently. By next spring most of these short stems will have dried out, but they'll still be visible as markers to show you where the plants are going to come up again.

As always, there are exceptions to this rule.

The tougher mat-forming perennials, such as *arabis albida, cerastium* (snow-in-summer), *iberis, lamium, phlox subulata* (rock phlox), *sedum spurium* and *stachys lanata* (lamb's ears) will keep most of their foliage quite nicely under the snow cover, bouncing back quickly in the spring. All you have to do is trim them back in the autumn to keep them in bounds. The same applies to ground covers such as *ajuga, convallaria, pachysandra* and *vinca.*

Another exception is the group of shrub-like vines such as *clematis* and *lonicera* (honeysuckle) that should be allowed to keep their stems for next year. These can be left to fend for themselves over the winter, as they will start to re-grow from the old stems as soon as the snow melts.

Digging and storing summer bulbs.

Back in the early summer you may have planted what are referred to as "summer bulbs". These are varieties such as agapanthus, tuberous begonia, caladium, calla lily, canna lily, crocosima, dahlia, eucomis, galtonia, gladiolus, gloriosa lily, incarvillia, kniphofia, tigridia and tuberose.

I am referring to all of these plants as summer "bulbs" for convenience, but in fact they are a collection of bulbs, tubers, corms and rhizomes.

They are unlike spring bulbs, because they can't tolerate the extremely cold temperatures of the winter, even underground. Most of them are only hardy to about zone 5, which means they are only hardy in Canadian locations like the Maritimes, the west coast and southern Ontario. Even in these places they need to be well mulched over the winter to protect them.

So in most places they have to be taken out of the ground and put away safely for the winter months (lifted and stored) until they can be planted again next season. By saving them you not only save money by not having to buy new ones each year, but you may also benefit by finding that they grow in size or grow additional bulbs that you can use.

Wait until the first frost kills off their foliage, then dig them out of the ground carefully with a garden fork, and shake off the excess soil. Take them indoors and lay them on sheets of newspaper to dry off overnight, with identification tags attached telling you the variety and colour. The next day, clean off the remaining soil and then trim off the leaves and stems close to the bulb. Dust each bulb with a sulphur-based fungicide to protect them from disease over the winter. Make sure the identification tags stay with each group of bulbs. Let them sit and dry completely for about 10 days, then brush them clean, ready for storage.

To store them until early next spring they need to be kept cool and dry. They should be stored in a temperature range of between 8 to 12 degrees C (45-55F), and never exposed to freezing.

An ideal way to store them is in wooden or plastic-foam boxes, spaced so they are not touching (to avoid the spread of any rot), and buried in dry peat moss or vermiculite. Cardboard boxes are acceptable, as long as they are kept where it is completely dry. Don't throw them into plastic bags or airtight containers as any moisture will be trapped inside and cause problems.

Protecting roses during the winter.
In regions where winter temperatures drop below minus 10 degrees C (14F), many roses are not hardy enough to withstand these conditions without some protection. The only roses that can over-winter naturally are non-hybrids which have not been grafted. These are usually referred to as "rugosa" or "hardy" roses, and they come in many forms from miniatures to climbers.

The part of a hybrid rose that is most susceptible to winter damage is the graft, or union, where the hybrid cultivar is grafted to a stronger root stock. During the winter, this union needs protecting. A good protection method is to cover the area of the graft just above the root crown with soil, compost, shredded bark or shredded leaves. These latter two materials can be blown away by the wind, so they should be surrounded by branches, cloth or a layer of soil to keep them in place.

Other winter damage can be caused under severe conditions to all types of roses, by the drying effects of the wind and the winter sun. Freezing wind can desiccate and kill exposed rose canes. Winter sun can actually warm up one side of a rose cane and cause it to split when it freezes again.

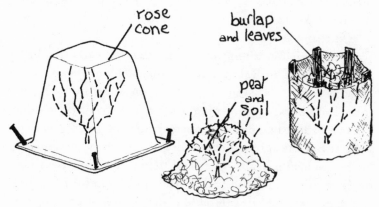

[FIG. 58] ROSE PROTECTION

This sort of wind and sun damage can only be protected against with a physical barrier. For the tougher hardy roses, a covering of snow is usually sufficient protection, but a hardy climber that's exposed above the snow can benefit from a cloth covering over its canes.

For hybrids, this exposure protection is essential. Use winter cloth, burlap or pre-formed plastic covers to hide the rose canes. [fig. 58] The new white winter cloth, which has a moisture-proof plastic coating on the outside and an insulating cloth coating in the inside, can be wrapped around individual plants or draped over whole rose beds to form a tent-like protection. Use a few strong sticks to support the weight of the snow, and to avoid the canes being eaten by rodents make sure to lay out packets of poisonous bait under the cloth covering.

Another fool-proof method of protecting large and small hybrids roses from winter damage is to bury them. This may seem extreme, but it really works. Use a fork to loosen the roots of the rose, and carefully dig it out and shake off all the earth. The stems can be left at any length, but they should be tied loosely together with twine. Dig a trench, six inches deep and as long as the combined length of the stems and roots. Lay the bare-rooted rose down in the trench, and fill it with either shredded leaves or peat moss, and cover the top with soil. Place sturdy markers at each end of the trench so that you can find it next spring.[fig. 59]

In the spring, when the soil has thawed, carefully dig up the buried rose bush. You'll notice that all along the stems will be buds ready to start growing. Soak the roots in water for a couple of hours, then re-plant the rose in the usual manner. This procedure may delay the normal start of your rose-growing season, but the minor delay will be more than compensated for by the health of the canes and the number of strong buds ready to grow. This method is particularly useful for hybrid climbers that face considerable exposure and are difficult to properly protect.

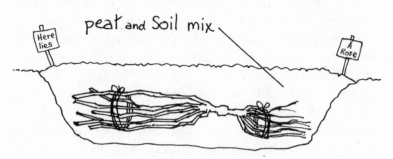

[FIG. 59] BURYING A ROSE

Over-wintering ornamental grasses.

All of the ornamental grasses that we use for decorative purposes are perennials, with strong root crowns that will start re-growing next spring.

But to give them a measure of protection over the winter and to ensure they build all the energy they can into their crowns, you should allow the autumn foliage to ripen and dry. Don't cut it down before the winter. With these varieties of ornamental grass there's no need to worry about their seed heads becoming a problem and spreading unchecked around your garden.

In the spring, as you see the small green shoots emerging from the root crown, you can trim off any dead leaves and stems to make the plant look tidy.

Besides, these often attractive clumps of foliage can become very interesting decoration in the winter garden.

Preparing the lawn for winter.

Speaking of grass, our lawns should be handled quite the oppo-site to ornamental grasses in the autumn. They should be cut quite short just prior to the first frost. This is to avoid having long grass blades die during the winter and form a heavy thatch.

Don't bother feeding the lawn in the autumn, as most of the nitrogen in the fertilizer will be washed away and wasted during the winter months. The only time to fertilize is if you've laid new sections of turf, and you want to encourage root growth with a potassium-rich fertilizer.

Lawns can be repaired in the early autumn, when heavy foot traffic is reduced. Sections with poor growth or which have suffered damage can be reseeded or turfed.

Leaves that have fallen from deciduous trees should be cleared off the lawn every few days. This will reduce the damage caused by grass being stifled and cut off from water and light by densely packed leaves. It will also reduce the proliferation of fungal diseases and pest eggs over-wintering in the soil.

Leaves that become trapped under a layer of snow all winter get compacted and matted down, forming an impene-trable barrier to proper drainage and air circulation. Patches of dead leaves are often the cause of a fungus that attacks grass during the late winter and early spring, referred to as ice mold. Keep raking them up, even after the lawn has frozen solid, until the snow falls. They can be shredded and recycled through the compost.

For more details of these lawn care techniques, see Chapter Six.

Clearing up leaves.

It's a lot of work every autumn, but it's a very good idea to clear up the deciduous leaves which fall on your garden.

In the previous section we dealt with the problems that can be caused by leaving fallen leaves on a lawn. The same thing applies to leaves falling on your garden.

A mass of compacted leaves can severely interfere with the flow of water and air into the soil of your beds. And once the snow falls, this compacted layer of leaves will become all but impenetrable to the melting snow in the spring.

There are also pest controls to be considered. Some of the fallen leaves may have been infected with fungus and will con-tain spores which can then over-winter in protected conditions to haunt you again next season. The same thing applies to the eggs and grubs of insects, which may become a pest next year.

Fallen leaves, if infected, should unfortunately be disposed of in the regular garbage. Uninfected leaves should be recycled into a compost system. If you don't have one of your own to handle large or small amounts of leaves (see Chapter Two), then forward the leaves to your municipal compost collection. If you don't have this service available, I'd suggest you pressure your municipal council to institute a leaf collection that's sent to a commercial compost site.

Protecting evergreen shrubs for the winter.

In a northern climate, evergreens which are native to the region don't need much protection. They slow their growth and go into a rest period, and their tough foliage is able to resist moisture loss due to winter wind and sun.

However, there are a few situations where evergreens need some protection during the winter.

An evergreen planted late in the season may have a small growth spurt once it's settled into place, and this new growth will not have time to harden off before the winter arrives. This new growth will likely get burned during the winter, and appear as brown tips in the spring. Just trim them off lightly with hedge shears to renew the look of the foliage.

An evergreen planted in a location that's exposed to a constant strong wind during the winter can have the youngest of its foliage burned. You can trim off the brown parts, but it might also be a good idea to provide a barrier to the winds as well. A section of snow fence or some stakes can be covered with a burlap screen to mollify the force of the prevailing wind, or the whole plant can be wrapped with burlap or winter cloth.

During our winters we can have some very mixed weather conditions, resulting in bouts of freezing rain and heavy wet snow. This puts an unexpected load on brittle evergreen branches, which can result in breakage. All that's needed is a little support. Tall columnar and short globular varieties can be held together by being wrapped with green twine from bottom to top to hold the branches together. Spreading varieties will need some sort of light framework over them to reduce the weight of what falls on them. These frames can be built from wood and nails, or purchased in clip-together sections that look rather like snow-fence.[fig.60]

Finally, evergreens planted close to buildings can be damaged by lumps of falling snow or ice, which break the branches apart. In this case what's needed is the same sort of wrapping or framework protection mentioned above for wet snow and ice.

[FIG. 60] PROTECTING EVERGREENS

There are a couple of broad-leafed evergreen varieties we grow in our gardens that also need a little protection. *Rhododendron* and the related *azalea* are one, and the other is *buxus*, better known as the Box plant.

These plants are evergreen in the sense that they keep their leaves all winter, but the leaves are not needles like their coniferous cousins. They are quite winter hardy, but for the sake of protecting their leaves from desiccation we should surround them with a wind-proof barrier. This could be made from winter cloth or burlap, and need only be wrapped around them with twine or stapled to wooden stakes.

Protecting deciduous shrubs for the winter.

The deciduous shrubs that are sold in our gardening regions are usually hardy enough to go through the winter without many problems. There are occasions where a gardener plants a shrub variety that is marginally hardy in their particular region, such as a *wisteria* vine, and it may succumb after a few winter seasons.

But about the only protection the hardy shrubs need for the winter is against damage caused by ice and snow.

Hedges can support each other against damage from weight by being tied in bunches. Grab a handful of bare branches, wrap some garden twine around the top third of them and then, without cutting the twine, move on to the next section and do the same. You'll create a series of teepees held together by twine that will all support each other.

Small to medium sized specimen shrubs can be protected in a similar way against the weight of freezing rain or wet snow on their bare branches. Use garden twine to gather the branches lightly, starting at the bottom of the shrub, and spiral it around the branches to the top. This will offer just enough support to withstand even the heaviest coating of ice.[fig. 61]

Very large deciduous shrubs, such as old lilac or mock orange (philadelphus) bushes have to take their chances with the vagaries of the weather. Any particularly weak or badly-angled branches could be supported with metal or wooden stakes, but if this is the case perhaps they should be shortened or removed entirely.

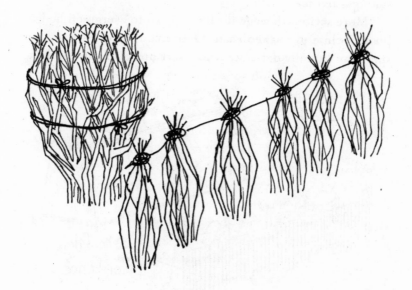

[FIG. 61] STRINGING HEDGES AND ROPING SHRUBS

Protecting your property from salt spray.
If you live alongside a road or highway which is regularly salted during the winter, and the traffic moves fast enough to cause a lot of spray to drift onto your property, then you may have faced damage from the salt spray.

It could be as moderate as some damage to the roadside edges of your lawn, or it could be eating away at your evergreen hedge. Salt can be a herbicide, killing all plants that it touches, so you may need some protection against it.

A small amount of surface damage to the blades of grass nearest a sidewalk or road can usually be neutralized by a heavy watering with a sprinkler in the early spring. Washing away the superficial salt and diluting it is usually enough in these cases. If your lawn edges are badly damaged, you may need to replace them with strips of turf. Sometimes the municipality has a budget for repairing this sort of winter damage caused by its salting activities.

More serious damage if often caused to evergreen hedges planted close to a salted road. Over a couple of years the salt spray can literally defoliate whole sections of plants, and the

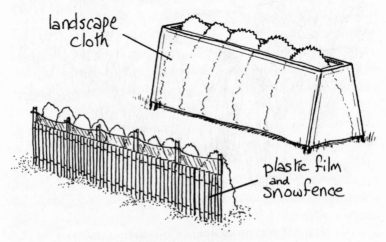

[FIG. 62] ANTI-SPRAY BARRIERS

only repair options are to add more shrubs in front of the hedge or replace them entirely. This still doesn't stop the spray from causing more damage.

The most sensible solution to this that I've seen so far is to set up a physical barrier against the spray. It requires something sturdy such as snow-fence laid against metal posts, with a layer of burlap or winter cloth attached behind the fence to catch the spray.[fig. 62] This is not a cheap solution, but it can be reused each winter for several years and is certainly better than the cost of continually replacing plants.

When to use winter mulch.

The idea of winter mulching is quite different from mulching during the summer. The latter is to keep moisture in the soil and to reduce the need to weed. Winter mulching, on the other hand, is to protect the plants in the ground from a particular damage due to the winter weather.

Sometimes our winter weather throws a series of freezing and thawing cycles at us, where periods of mild weather can come in the middle of the cold season. The ground has time to thaw slightly on the surface, and then freezing temperatures return and make the ground hard again. This has the unfortunate effect of shrinking and expanding wet soil as the moisture alternately thaws and freezes.

This can become a real problem for plants that are trying to quietly survive the winter. For example, the soil that has been disturbed in the autumn where bulbs or perennials were planted is a different texture or structure to the surrounding soil, so it absorbs more water. When the thaw and freeze cycle comes along, this "plug" of moist disturbed soil can literally get heaved out of the ground as it contracts and expands. Plant roots can be exposed, bulbs can be uncovered and all sorts of damage can ensue.

To avoid this situation, we use a winter mulch. It uses the same materials as for a summer mulch, such as shredded bark or straw, but it has to be applied at just the right time. The idea is to keep the soil under the mulch *frozen* all winter long, so it should only be applied after the ground has frozen hard in the late autumn or early winter.

This also ensures that rodents don't use your mulch as a home for the winter.

With the ground frozen and the mulch in place, no matter what weather comes along, the ground will stay frozen solid and they won't run the risk of being disturbed.

Winter mulch should be applied over areas where you have planted bulbs, surrounding newly-planted perennials or shrubs and around perennials which are marginally hardy such as Shasta daisies and lavender.

Preparing the soil for the winter.

All summer your plants have been taking nutrients out of the flower and vegetable gardens, and the organisms in the soil have been breaking down the organic matter and turning it into humus. So these things need to be replaced, ready for next year. You can add all sorts of soil amendments in the autumn and they will work their way into the soil over the winter, to replenish and refresh it.

In the flower garden, spread some organic matter around the root areas of your perennials. Shredded leaves are good, and they can be obtained simply by running your lawn mower over rows of raked leaves on the lawn and collecting the output. Chopped straw is also very suitable, and bales of it are often available right after Halloween from neighbourhood decorations. Once you've spread this loosely, you can hold it in place by spreading compost (either home-made or purchased) on top of it.

Don't bother spreading fertilizers in the autumn flower garden. With so little growth happening, the plants are not in any need of it.

In the vegetable garden, there's work to be done to amend

the soil for next year. Start by spreading as much organic matter as you can over the vegetable beds, and then as much compost as you can spare as well. Adding a handful of horticultural lime for every square foot of bed will raise the calcium and magnesium level. You can also apply nutrient sources that are slow to break down, such as granite dust or wood ash (potassium) and rock phosphate or bone meal (phosphor).

Once all of these additions have been spread on the soil surface, lightly turn over the soil with a spade and leave the soil in clumps. This will expose more surface area to the weathering effects of the winter, and by the spring a lot of what you spread will be incorporated into the soil.

Tidying up the garden area.

Just before you walk away from the garden for the winter season, there are probably a couple of jobs to be looked after to make sure things are in good shape next spring.

It's a good idea to drain all hoses and irrigation systems before the first frost, to avoid any damage from ice. Most of the new semi-rigid plastic hoses can withstand a certain amount of ice inside them, but small emitters and connectors may not be so robust. Drain them to the lowest point in the system, and reseal the system to avoid any animal life entering it. Taps from inside water supplies which are mounted outdoors should also be drained and closed. Garden hoses should be drained and stored indoors for the winter, to avoid unnecessary deterioration of the material. The same applies to sprinklers and water timers.

Garden furniture may need protecting or putting away, which will depend from what material it's made. Plastics and synthetic composites will last many more years if they're not exposed to freezing temperatures, so they should be brought indoors. Wooden furniture is more forgiving, but to avoid premature deterioration and discoloration from molds it can be covered with plastic fabric or brought indoors. Painted metal furniture is tough, but ferrous metals could do with a coating of preservative spray to avoid rust spots.

Have one last look around for any tools that you might have laid down as you worked with them, so they don't have to spend the winter outdoors.

NINE

Tools

A good gardener needs good tools.

That doesn't mean you require a huge arsenal of flashy ones. In fact, some of your favourite tools are probably old and scarred from many a battle with the soil. Most gardening chores are made easier by using the correct tool for the job. So depending on the size of your garden and the type of work you do regularly, you should have a few of the basic necessities.

Gardening, like other hobbies, attracts its fair share of people inventing new gadgets, not all of which are worth buying. In this chapter we'll try to sort out what tools you really need for your style of gardening.

Does it matter what tools are made of?

The composition of a garden tool or the finish on its surface can have an effect on the way it works. This usually means paying more for a tool to get better quality. But my experience has been that a better-quality tool not only works better, it lasts longer too.

Digging tools have to slide through the soil, which can be filled with stones and roots. For this you obviously need a sharp edge, but the surface finish can also be important. The very shiny stainless steel or high-carbon steel tools have a strong surface that resists pitting and scratching, and they almost glide into the soil with very little effort. Compare this to the rough finish of a cheaper version of the same tool, and after using both you'll soon see the difference in effort required.

The same thing applies to cutting tools. A blade that takes

and holds a sharp edge with only minimal honing will make pruning work a lot easier on the hands than one that becomes blunt more quickly. Whether it's a saw or pruning shear, hardened steel blades of an almost surgical quality may cost a bit more, but the ease of use and upkeep is usually worth the difference.

The type of handle on a tool can also make a difference. Wooden handles on digging tools should be made of a flexible but strong wood such as ash, as was used in early longbows. This gives strength as well as the ability to absorb the shock that accompanies digging. Smaller tools often use hickory to get the same shock-dampening effect along with strength. There are also modern composite materials that mimic this action for tool handles.

In hand tools, particularly the smaller ones, the latest trend is to design them ergonomically. The shape of the handle and the materials it's made from reduce the strain and effort of long-tem use. This usually means a handle that's bent to keep the wrist at a more comfortable angle, as well as being shaped to fit the hand better. Some also use softer materials for the hand grip, to reduce the effort required to hold the tool clamped steadily. [fig. 63]

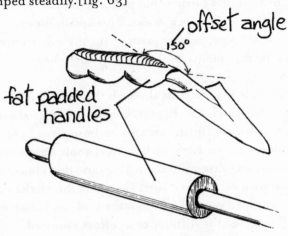

offset angle

150°

fat padded handles

[FIG. 63] ERGONOMIC HANDLES

What small digging tools are absolutely essential?

Even if all you have are some containers on a balcony, you'll need a basic planting tool. A **trowel** will serve several purposes. It can dig planting holes, but it can also be used to scoop soil and stir it up. There are trowels with serrated edges for cutting through light roots, wide or narrow ones for making different-sized holes and others that are shaped to hold soil like a scoop. Some oriental-style diggers (ho-mi) have their pointed blade at right angles to the handle, which is useful for digging shallow trenches. And ergonomics have changed the look of even the traditional trowel, to make it more comfortable to use. So you may end up having a few different trowels to be used for different purposes.[fig. 64]

Hand tools are often sold in sets, with a **weeding fork** included. Because I use a lot of mulch I don't do a lot of weeding,

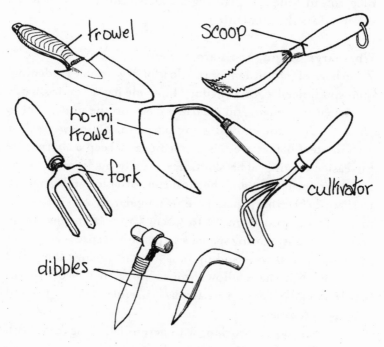

[FIG. 64] HAND TOOLS

so I don't find it necessary to have one as part of my kit. But they can be useful in loosening compacted soil and digging out perennial weeds.

Another tool often included in a set is a **cultivator**. This looks like a sharp-pointed claw with three or four tines, used to scratch the soil surface and loosen it to make pulling annual weeds easier. Again, by using a lot of mulch I avoid a lot of weeding. Besides, this sort of constant cultivating disturbs the structure of the soil and causes moisture to evaporate faster.

One of the most useful tools I have for making holes is a **giant dibble**. It has a T-shaped handle, and the 12-inch long aluminum shaft is fat enough that it makes a perfect-sized hole for dropping in annuals. My grandfather used something similar, made from the handle-end of a broken spade, cut to about a foot long. The two-inch wide wooden shaft made a nice round hole for planting annuals, and this new metal version does the same thing.

What large digging tools are needed?

If you have a large garden, or you do a lot of vegetable gardening, then you'll need a good **spade**. The spade has a flat or slightly curved cutting edge, and a narrow tread on the upper end to place the foot for extra digging pressure. Stainless steel or carbon-steel blades are the strongest, and keep a sharp edge for easier digging. The shafts are usually made of wood or composite materials, and the most comfortable hand-grips are D-shaped. Ordinary spades are rectangular, from six to eight inches across and from 23 to 30cm (9 to 12 inches) long. However, transplanting spades and perennial spades are about 13cm (5 inches) wide and up to 45cm (18 inches) long, and this long thin shape allows you to work in narrow spaces between plants. They are particularly useful when digging and moving perennials.

Another tool for working with perennials is the **fork**. With three or four tines, they are in the same size ranges as the ordinary spades, and made of the same materials. They are most useful for loosening the soil under large clumps of perennials or when digging up vegetables. Forks with flat tines are usually used for heavy digging and turning soil, whereas ones with round ones are normally for loosening the soil.

If you move a lot of loose material, such as soil or gravel, you should have a **shovel** to do it. This tool is almost the same as the spade mentioned before, but it has a slightly concave sharply curved heart-shaped blade. Rather than for digging, it is designed to scoop into loose material and carry a load without spilling it. Some shovels have long straight handles which make it easier to throw and spread materials.[fig. 65]

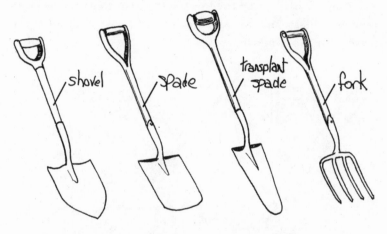

[FIG. 65] LARGE DIGGING TOOLS

How many rakes are needed?
If you have a lot of exposed soil, such as in a vegetable garden, then you should have a **soil rake**. The hard teeth of this rake will help you level lumps of soil after digging, for making a smooth seed bed and it's also useful when spreading soil on a lawn. It's good for collecting stones from the soil surface that are larger than the spaces between its tines. Pulling the rake towards you collects things, pushing it away helps to break things

up. You can even turn it over and use the back to flatten or smooth soil evenly. Soil rakes are usually 25 to 30cm (10 to 12 inches) wide, although some narrower ones are available for working between existing plants.

Anyone with a lawn or with trees nearby needs a **lawn rake**. They usually have a fan-shaped spread of flexible tines, and are used for collecting leaves or debris without disturbing the surface underneath. Metal tines are more durable than bamboo, but many lawn rakes are now made from plastic compositions. On behalf of many of your neighbours, please keep using a lawn rake rather than switching to a leaf blower. The blowers may make your life easier, but they are rather noisy, and they are often used to blow the leaves onto someone else's property. Please, use the rake (for the exercise), and gather the leaves (for the compost).

[FIG. 66] RAKE STYLES

What about tools for weed control?

The best weapon against weeds is a thick layer of mulch (see Chapter 4). Using tools to remove annual weed seedlings runs certain risks. You disturb the soil and raise dormant weed seeds to the surface, you break up the soil structure and you encourage the evaporation of moisture.

However, if you insist upon using a tool for weed control, the following are useful.

The traditional way of destroying small weeds in the soil is to chop them down with a **hoe**. The sharp blade slices through the weed stems at ground level and kills them. There are several styles of hoe, and the choice is one of preference rather than function. All have long straight handles to reach a good distance without bending. The blade should be positioned to work parallel to the surface, so it glides back and forth on or just under the soil.[fig. 67]

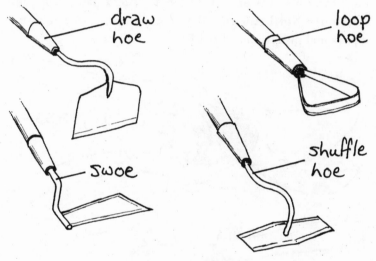

[FIG. 67] HOE STYLES

Another form of weed control uses a **cultivator claw**, similar to the hand cultivator, but on the end of a long straight handle. It scratches the soil and disturbs the weeds, but suffers from the same drawbacks as mentioned before with the hand version.

There are several patented cultivation gadgets, based on spiked wheels or claws that need to be inserted into the soil and then twisted. In my opinion these are worse for the soil than other cultivation techniques, and should be avoided.

How many pruning tools are needed?

There are two main types of tools used for pruning operations, shears and saws. Within each type are different sizes to handle different diameters of wood.

With most types of shears there are two styles of blade configurations, **bypass** and **anvil**. The bypass has a blade on top that slides past a lower non-cutting arm which holds the wood in place. It gives a clean cut, but can be forced apart by very tough wood. The anvil has a blade on top, which presses down onto a flat soft-metal surface. It doesn't get forced apart, but it can crush the end of the wood. The bypass is the most common in North America, the anvil in Europe, so it's a matter of personal preference. [fig. 68]

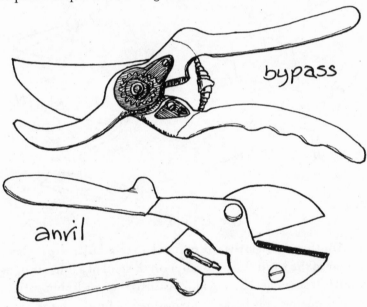

[FIG. 68] PRUNING SHEAR STYLES

The smallest pruning tool is the **pruning shear,** used to cut wood up to 2cm (3/4 inch) in diameter. The handles are usually spring-loaded to keep the blades open, and some models rotate slightly as you squeeze them to ease the strain on the hand or have a ratchet-action which increases the cutting leverage. Pruning shears come in several sizes, and some styles are more suited to cutting flowers than branches.

A slightly larger shear is called a **lopping shear**, and is good for wood up to 5cm (2 inches) in diameter. It has the same style of cutting action as a pruning shear, but has long handles

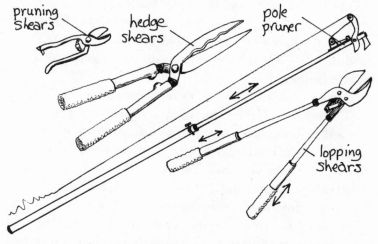

[FIG. 69] DIFFERENT TYPES OF SHEARS

from 38 to 60cm (15 to 24 inches) to provide extra leverage. There are bypass and anvil style blades, and they may include ratchet-action operation to make it easier on the arms. They are also useful for working in tall shrubs and small trees because of their longer reach.

You might not think of trimming a hedge as pruning, but it certainly is, since you're removing foliage to guide the way a plant grows. For this work, you'll need a pair of **hedge shears,** like giant scissors, with blades at least 20cm (8 inches) long to cut a wide but even swath and with similarly long handles to give good leverage. The repetitive nature of this clipping work can soon tire your hands and arms, so soft thick handles will help.

For very large amounts of hedge work you'd be advised to use a **power hedge trimmer**, usually electric, which slices rather than clips the foliage.

For very high pruning work there's the **pole pruner**. This has a bypass-style blade on the end of a long pole, and the cutting action is operated by a rope and pulley system. The upper part of the blade is hooked over the branch to be cut, the rope is pulled downwards and the lower blade cuts the branch. It works on wood up to about 5cm (2 inches) thick. Some pole pruners also have a pruning saw attached on the end. You only need this tool if you have very tall shrubs or small trees you want to prune.

For pruning off wood that's thicker than 5cm (2 inches) you'll need to use some type of saw. A **pruning saw** should have a slightly curved blade, so it avoids snagging other wood when it is used. The blades are designed to only cut on the pull stroke, unlike carpentry saws. The easiest to use are under 60cm (2 feet) long, and they should have a comfortable handle. Some are made to fold into the handle for ease of carrying.

Working by hand on wood that's thicker than 76cm (3 inches) requires a **bow saw**. It has a thin blade which is stretched tight on a metal frame, and its long teeth cut on both the pull and the push strokes. It removes large chips on each stroke,

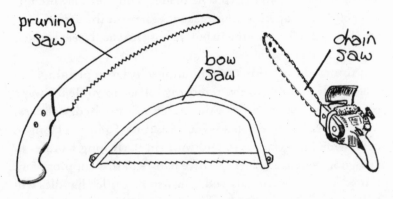

[FIG. 70] SAW TYPES

and can be used on wood up to about 12cm (5 inches).

For pruning requiring the cutting of wood thicker than 12cm (5 inches), or where a lot of heavy work has to be done, then a power-operated **chain saw** is really needed. These require careful handling, as gasoline-powered saws operate at high speeds and cut quickly, with the risk of the whole blade bucking back at your body if it encounters difficulty while cutting.[fig. 70] A new series of electrically-powered chain saws are now available that are easier to handle, some of which have protective sheaths over the blades and are used rather like a pair of giant shears.

I find it essential to have a couple of really sharp **knives** on hand at all times. I use an old kitchen knife with an 18cm (7 inch) blade to chop through roots when I'm dividing perennials. I also have a short-bladed utility knife to cut lengths of twine and to trim off ragged wood when I'm pruning. There are also special knives for grafting and pruning work, with blade shapes which make the work easier.

How do you keep cutting tools sharp?

There's absolutely no point in having a cutting tool of any kind unless it's kept sharp. A blunt tool will not only cause you fatigue or muscle strain, it will also damage the item it's cutting.

The general rule is that the finer the edge on the tool, the finer the device needed to keep it sharp.

The cutting edge on a spade or shovel should be kept sharp and free of gouges, so it can slice through the soil. Use a mill file to establish a well-formed edge.

The blades of knives and shears of all sizes don't actually need to be "sharpened" regularly. They just need to be "honed" to re-establish their cutting edge. Honing only requires a gentle amount of work to realign the molecules of the metal. For the fine edges of shears you can use a ceramic, diamond or aluminum oxide hone, which is usually part of a flat or rod-shaped tool. You stroke the blade downwards in a cutting motion at a slight angle to the hone, **not** parallel to the blade. Think of it as straightening out the molecules to all point in lines away from the edge of the blade.[fig. 71]

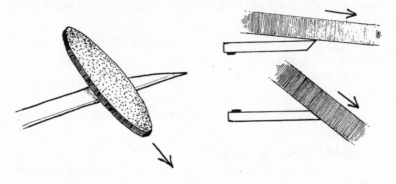

[FIG. 71] HONING EDGES

Hone all of your cutting edges *after* you've used them, so they will be ready to use right away next time you need them. Clean off any plant saps with alcohol, and then rub the metal with a thin coat of light machine oil.

Hand saw blades stay sharp a lot longer than shears, but eventually need attention too. You can use special handsaw files, or take them to a professional saw sharpener once every few years.

Chainsaw blades need sharpening when the wood they remove changes from small distinct chips to sawdust. This is a sign the blade is grinding the wood rather than cutting it. You can buy chainsaw sharpening kits, or use a professional sharpening service.

Always be careful when sharpening and handling cutting edges. Use leather or Kevlar-coated gloves when doing any pruning work. Position the cutting tool first, pause to consider where your hands and all of your fingers are, and then start the cut.

What lawn tools are needed?

Just to cut your grass you'll need a **mower**, but as I mentioned in Chapter Six, the best choice is a "reel" mower.

To trim the edges of your lawn where they come up against soil beds you can use either long or short-handled **lawn shears**.[fig. 72] They trim off the excess blades of grass that get missed by the mower right on the edge of the lawn. The long-handled ones can be used standing up rather than kneeling.

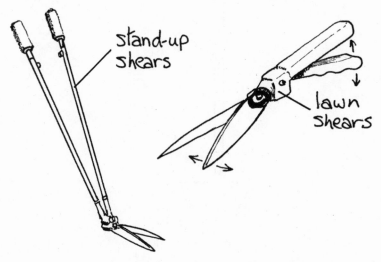

[FIG. 72] LAWN EDGING SHEARS

Another way of keeping the difficult areas of your lawn cut is with a **wire trimmer**. These electric or gasoline powered tools use a fast-spinning piece of plastic wire to slice grass blades. They are useful for lawn edges, for meadows with long grass and for places where it's difficult for a mower to go. Be careful with them around trees, as they can strip off the bark all around a trunk (girdling) which stops the flow of sap. You can cover the base of a tree with plastic or a metal tree guard to protect against this.

If you have a lawn with a lot of flower beds next to it, you'll find the **edging iron** or **edging spade** very useful. [fig. 73] This tool has a shaft and handle like a spade, but its blade is a half-moon with a sharp rounded edge. It's used to trim off sections of lawn roots that encroach into the flower beds, and should be sliced into the soil at a slight angle leaning away from the bed. As an alternative, you can use a sharp spade.

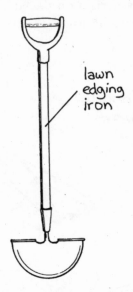

lawn edging iron

[FIG. 73] LAWN EDGING IRON

Some other tools that may be useful.

If you make and move a lot of compost, a **manure fork** is useful. It usually has from five to ten tines set slightly curved and quite close together, to make gathering and loading easier. Sometimes the tines have round protective balls on their tips rather than points, because these tools are often used around the feet of animals.

Over the years, several designs of **rock rakes** have been made. They have half a dozen long, very closely-spaced tines, either at right angles to the handle or in the shape of a basket. They are very useful for working stony soils where a lot of debris has to be removed.

If you do a lot of planting from seed, you'll spend a lot of time each spring preparing your seed beds. Nothing makes this work easier than a **soil sieve**. They are available in various mesh sizes to create a fine particle size, or "tilth," which is essential for outdoor seed planting.

Also useful when planting a lot of vegetable seeds are gadgets to set the planting distance and depth for the seeds. You can make **seed guides** first of all with string and two wooden stakes to make sure you plant in straight rows. Other guides can be made from lengths of wood with nails or pegs set at the correct distance and depth, to make planting holes for each type of seed.

Working around any garden, you're bound to pull out weeds and pick up debris as you go. To keep this from becoming a mess, take a **garden bag** along with you at all times. Rather than a plastic garbage bag, which never stays open when you want it to, these polypropylene bags hold their shape and stay open even when empty. Just dump them into the compost when you're finished.

With all of the tools that you need as you patrol your garden, it's always useful to have some sort of **tool carrier**. Whether it's a belt with assorted pockets, a plastic tub or bag full of hand tools or a wheeled device to hold all of your large and small tools, a carrier lets you have them when you need them and it keeps them all together.

Speaking of wheels, the larger your garden the more likely you are to need a **wheelbarrow** of some sort. Whether it's the traditional single-wheeled style, or the newer ones with two large bicycle-type wheels, wheelbarrows have a large number of uses. From carrying loads of lose materials to bringing plants to where they're to be planted, a barrow saves a lot of back-breaking work. [fig. 74]

Any garden is going to need at least one **hose**, and I'd highly recommend you buy either a 5/8 inch or ¾ inch diameter size,

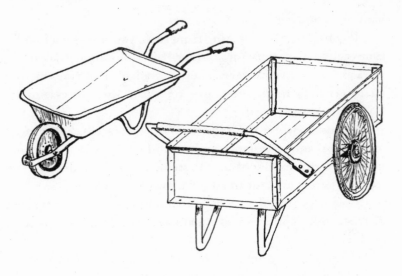

[FIG. 74] WHEELBARROWS

in a multi-layer construction. They are less likely to kink, and won't burst or split. Some are even advertised as guaranteed to last a "lifetime". You should also gradually switch all of your hose attachments from plastic to brass, as it's more durable and will last virtually forever.

There will probably be some places where a hose won't reach, so a **watering can** will always be helpful. Whether it's metal or plastic, it should have a capacity between about four to six litres. Any smaller and it requires frequent filling, any larger and it gets too heavy to handle.

What sort of care and maintenance do tools need?

Metal digging tools should always be cleaned after use, to remove moisture and soil traces that could stain or rust the metal. Wipe them with a brush or spray them with water to clean, then dry them with a soft cloth or paper towel. For tools where a painted surface gets worn away to expose bare metal, the metal should be given a thin coating of light machine oil to resist rust. At the end of the season, all metal surfaces should be treated this way before storage.

Wooden handles and parts should also be kept clean after each use, by wiping with a damp cloth. Follow this with a light application of linseed or tung oil to protect the surface of the wood and reduce shrinkage.

Synthetic materials can be cleaned with a brush and some soap and water. They seldom need further protection.

Metal cutting surfaces should be cleaned with alcohol to remove plant sap and sharpened after every use.

Moving parts where metal touches metal should be kept lubricated. For small tools, a light machine oil is suitable. For machinery, the manufacturer's instructions will tell you the frequency and type of lubrication needed.

TEN

Calendar

There's an inherent difficulty in setting up a gardening activity calendar for readers in several different regions across the country. Things such as planting dates vary by location, and won't be accurate everywhere.

To avoid confusion I've assumed a "safe" outdoor planting date for tender plants of May 24. Anything marked with an asterisk (*) is based upon this date. Yours may be sooner or later than this, in which case you should adjust the starting dates accordingly.

I've also assumed the first killing frost will come around November 15, so your autumn chores should take that into account as well.

January
Place seed orders (new seed varieties are often in short supply, so get your order in early)

February
*Plant seeds of perennials indoors
Re-start feeding houseplants monthly

March
*Plant seeds of annuals indoors
Take cuttings of over-wintered plants
*Plant seeds of large vegetables indoors
Maintenance prune shrubs/small trees

April

*Plant summer bulbs indoors
*Plant seeds of small vegetables indoors
Remove winter mulch (allowing soil to warm)
Remove winter protection from shrubs/evergreens
Maintenance prune shrubs/small trees (if not done)
Lawn maintenance when ground is dry (weeding, feeding, seeding)
Prepare compost pile for summer
Warm up vegetable beds for early planting
Feed spring bulbs

May

Prepare soil for planting, add amendments
*Start hardening-off seedlings grown indoors
*Plant seeds of cold-tolerant vegetables outdoors
*Deadhead spring bulbs
*Plant containers
*Plant new shrubs, perennials, herbs
*Divide/transplant perennials
Spray fruit trees (dormant oil, sulphur)
*Mulch exposed soil once it has warmed
*Plant seedlings outdoors (May 24)
Clip hedges

June

*Plant tender summer bulbs outdoors
*Plant seeds of remaining vegetables outdoors
Deadhead spring-flowering shrubs
Prune shrubs
Clip evergreen hedges
Cut back spring bulb foliage once ripe
Bring houseplants outdoors
Apply protective fungicide to affected plants
Apply lawn grub controls
Deadhead early perennials

July
Stake tall flowers and vegetables
Feed containers
Feed large vegetables
Deadhead perennials
Many, many other little things!

August
Buy/order spring bulbs
Plant new perennials
Plant seeds of late season vegetable crops
Feed containers
Feed large vegetables
Harvest some herbs
Pinch tomato plants (forcing fruit to ripen)
Last evergreen hedge trim before winter
Divide irises
Deadhead perennials

September
Divide/transplant early perennials
Plant spring bulbs (end of month)
Plant new shrubs
Plant onions/garlic
Feed containers
Deadhead perennials
Harvest all herbs
Bring houseplants indoors
Bring tender plants indoors (such as geraniums you wish to
    over-winter for cuttings)

October
Plant spring bulbs
Dig up annuals
Dig up vegetable garden

Dig up and store summer bulbs
Cut down perennials
Divide/transplant late perennials
Prune back tender plants brought indoors (use the tips for cuttings if desired)
Keep lawn free of leaves
Mow lawn bi-weekly until frost
Collect compost, prepare pile for winter
Add amendments to soil
Dig over vegetable bed
Plant amaryllis bulbs for holiday season (takes approx. 8 weeks to bloom).

November
Protect delicate shrubs (roses, rhododendrons, etc)
Protect shrubs against winter
Apply winter mulch once ground is frozen
Keep lawn & garden free of leaves
Stop feeding houseplants
Put away tools
Prepare indoor garden space

December
Plant paperwhite bulbs for holiday season (takes 2 weeks to bloom)
Order seed catalogues (if you want the actual books.) You can also go on-line to see the new varieties, but some suppliers may not be ready until January.
Plant spring bulbs indoors for forcing (takes approx. 10-15 weeks to bloom).

Glossary

Don't you hate it when people use terminology that you don't understand? Every hobby and profession has its jargon and its technical words, and they often make it hard to understand just what is being said.

Gardening is no different, and I abase myself if I've been culpable of obfuscation. In an attempt to make things a bit easier, here's a glossary of some of the activities and items you'll hear referred to quite often in this book.

Annual A plant that grows from seed to maturity in one season.

Biennial A plant that flowers and seeds in the second season from seed germination.

Bed An open area of soil used for planting. Often cut from a grassy area.

Crown The upper part of a root from which the shoots grow, and where they die back to in winter. Also, the upper branching part of a tree.

Cultivating Disturbing the surface of the soil, usually with a tool such as a hoe or a cultivator. Designed to kill sprouting weeds, it's an activity I recommend avoiding, because it actually spoils the structure of the soil and releases stored moisture to the air (see **Mulching**).

Dead-heading Removing flowers that have finished blooming. If left on the plant, they will set seeds and thereby slow the growth of the plant.

Dividing Digging up and cutting sections of plants, most often perennials, to renovate a clump or to multiply it. Divided sections can be transplanted elsewhere (see **Transplanting**).

Drip line A line on the soil under a tree where the rain water drips off the outermost leaves. Below this is the area with the most feeder root activity.

Edging Trimming the edge of a lawn with a sharp spade, shears or patented tool to stop grass roots from growing into a bed.

Fertilizing Adding selected nutrients to the soil that will dissolve and provide plants with food. The main elements are; nitrogen (N) for stem and leaf growth, phosphor (P) to develop strong root systems as well as flower and fruit growth, and potassium (K) that is mainly responsible for tissue strength, disease resistance and fruit development. The ratio of NPK is always listed on a fertilizer package, e.g. 5-10-5. Carbon, hydrogen and oxygen are essential too, but are available from the air. Other nutrients needed in small quantities are calcium and magnesium. Only trace amounts of boron, chlorine, copper, iron, manganese, molybdenum, sulphur and zinc are needed.

Foliar feeding Spraying a weak solution of liquid fertilizer on the foliage of a plant. Best done mid-season on large plants to assist growth. A recommended use for dilute "manure tea," made by soaking a sack of manure in a bucket of water overnight. Foliar feeding should be done in conjunction with feeding the soil (see **Fertilizing**).

Germination When a seed starts to grow and splits open to produce a root and a stem.

Heading back Pruning the tips of shrub and tree branches to stop further growth. This will result in a more dense growth of side shoots and foliage at the outer edges of the plant (see **Thinning**).

Hardening-off Toughening up plants (usually seedlings) that have been grown under cover, so that they can be planted outdoors with no risk of shock. Consists of gradual exposure to sun, wind, rain and outdoor temperature flucuations.

Layering Growing roots on a section of a plant's stem. Usually done on the hard wood of shrubs by bending the branch to the ground, breaking the branch slightly near the end, and burying the break in the soil. Roots will grow from the break, and the end of the branch can then be cut off and planted elsewhere.

Mulching Covering exposed soil with a blanket of some other material. This stops moisture evaporating from the soil, and chokes weed germination and growth. Common mulches are shredded wood, bark chips, grass clippings, cocoa bean hulls, straw, plastic film, spun fibre sheets, shredded newspaper. It reduces the need for weeding and watering (see **Cultivating**)

Node The point on a plant stem from where a leaf or stem will grow. The sections between nodes are inter-nodes.

Perennial A plant that lasts through many seasons.

Pinching Cutting off the very growing tip of a stem, often done with the thumb nail and forefinger. Similar to **Heading**. This slows tip growth and forces new growth to sprout from behind the cut, resulting in denser, more compact growth. Useful on annuals and perennials to encourage more flower heads.

Root pruning Trimming a quantity of the roots off a plant. Normally done to encourage new root growth in containerized plants, or to prepare a large soil-bound plant to be moved. When pruning off roots, a similar quantity of foliage should be removed to avoid stress to the plant.

Shrub A plant with many woody stems growing out of the ground, rather than one single stem.

Thinning Pruning out whole branches from a shrub or tree, to relieve congested growth. Usually the oldest branches are removed first. This results in a more open structure and stronger growth of the remaining branches (see **Heading**)

Top dressing Spreading fertilizer on the surface around a plant, without disturbing the plant roots, so that watering and rain will wash it into the soil. Use slow-release granular fertilizer, liquid fertilizer or compost. Side dressing is doing the same, but on either side of a plant.

Transplanting Moving a plant or section of a plant into a new location. Care must be taken to prepare the new planting hole with a suitable soil mix and moisture supply to encourage new root growth. Transplanting is best done in early spring or late fall when plants are less active and temperature stress is lower.

References

I owe these authors a debt of gratitude for the things they have taught me about gardening.

Bennett, J., "Dryland Gardening," Firefly Books, Ontario, 2005.

Biles, R.E.: "The Complete Book of Gardening Magic," J.G. Ferguson, Illinois, 1946.

Borrer, D.J., and DeLong, D.M.: "An Introduction to the Study of Insects," Saunders College Publishing, Texas, 1989.

Christopher, E.P.: "Introductory Horticulture," McGraw-Hill Book Company Inc., New York, 1958.

Cranshaw, W.: "Garden Insects of North America," Princeton University Press, New Jersey, 2004.

Cutting, A.B.: "Canadian Home Gardening" Second Edition, The Musson Book Company, Ontario, 1951.

Ellis, B.W., and Bradley, F.M.: "Natural Insect and Disease Control," Rodale Press, Pennsylvania, 1992.

Gustafson, A.F.: "Using and Managing Soils," McGraw-Hill Book Company Inc., New York, 1948.

Hendrix, H., and Straw, S.: "Reliable Rain," The Taunton Press, Connecticut, 1998.

Huxley, A.: "Encyclopedia of Gardening," Penguin Books Ltd., Middlesex, 1981.

Martin, D.L., and Gershuny, G.: "The Rodale Book of Composting," Rodale Press, Pennsylvania, 1992.

Ortloff, H.S., and Raymore, H.B.: "A Book About Soils,"

William Morrow & Company Inc, New York, 1962.

Reilly, A.: "Success with Seeds," George W. Park Seed Company, South Carolina, 1978.

Thompson, L.M.: "Soils and Soil Fertility," McGraw-Hill Book Company Inc., New York, 1952.

Vick, E.C., "Audels Gardeners and Growers Guide," Audel & Co., New York, 1928.

Westcott, C.: "The Gardener's Bug Book," Fourth Edition, Doubleday & Company, New York, 1972.

Index

This book has been printed on 100% post consumer
waste paper, certified Eco-logo and processed chlorine free.